The Complete

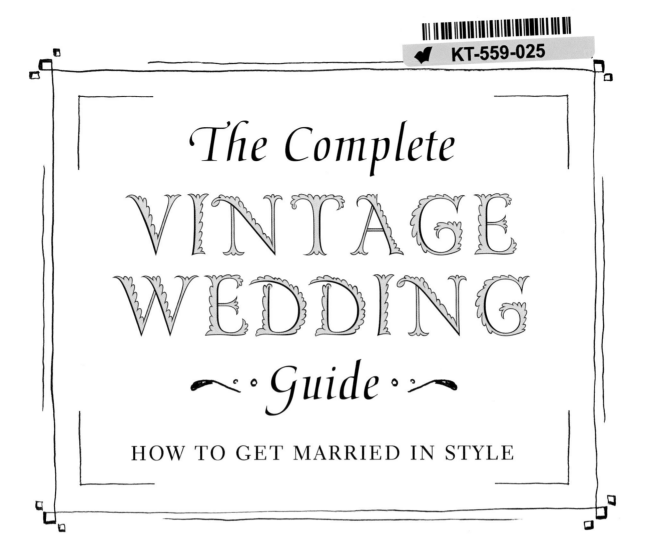

VINTAGE WEDDING

~ Guide ~

HOW TO GET MARRIED IN STYLE

~ Lucy Morris ~

Photography by Joanna Millington

D&C
David and Charles

www.stitchcraftcreate.co.uk

CONTENTS

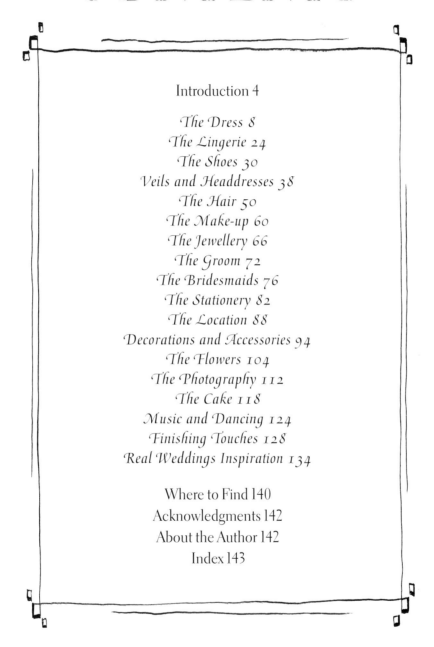

Introduction 4

The Dress 8
The Lingerie 24
The Shoes 30
Veils and Headdresses 38
The Hair 50
The Make-up 60
The Jewellery 66
The Groom 72
The Bridesmaids 76
The Stationery 82
The Location 88
Decorations and Accessories 94
The Flowers 104
The Photography 112
The Cake 118
Music and Dancing 124
Finishing Touches 128
Real Weddings Inspiration 134

Where to Find 140
Acknowledgments 142
About the Author 142
Index 143

← *The bride wears a 1950s gold and cream lace dress, with brown and cream peep-toe shoes and a 1940s cream sequined silk hat. The groom wears an Old Town tie, a vintage waistcoat and pin-striped navy blue trousers.*

Dedication

For my husband Kevin and our children Ottilie, Rufus and Agatha. Also for my inspirational and beautiful Mother, who taught me the difference between fashion and style.

INTRODUCTION

WHAT do we actually mean by this term 'vintage', which has swept the nation and is applied to everything from lampshades to lollipops? For me it has become a byword for something broader and more interesting than the confines of the word suggests. It is about personal expression, charm, perhaps a little eccentricity and a gentle nod to the old-fashioned. It doesn't mean that everything has to be old and dated or terribly 'war time'. When executed to perfection and with a lightness of touch, vintage style can be whimsical, elegant and can sit happily alongside the contemporary.

↑ *What a dress, what a bouquet, what a necklace! From the wedding of Emily and Jo Flatt, East Anglian Railway Museum, Colchester.*

↑ *This couple are photographed in one of the beautiful and individual rooms at Voewood House. Clothes as described previously.*

I don't claim to be an authority on wedding fashion through the ages and shan't pretend that my familiarity with wedding ceremony etiquette in the 1900s extends beyond a passing interest. However, it is with a passionate attention to detail, coupled with a love of beautiful things – ranging in breadth from hairgrips, buttons and stripy paper straws to English country gardens and exquisite handmade lace – that I share my ideas with you in this book. I am intensely aware that the planning of the visual extravaganza that is your wedding day is a daunting and exciting task in equal measure, and that it is the opportunity of a lifetime to visually express who you are and how you feel before you even utter a word. I hope therefore that the advice and expertise you find in these pages will give you the inspiration and bravado to weave charming vintage details into your wedding day to make it the most enchanting and memorable occasion for you and your wedding throng.

Following a number of years running a successful vintage crockery and accessories hire company, I have gathered a wealth of experience and information on planning a vintage event. This book is dedicated to the unearthing of unique suppliers of vintage finery for your wedding day – everything from where and how to buy the perfect vintage wedding dress, to beautiful ideas for place settings, favours, flower arrangements, stationery and so much more. There is even a chapter on real weddings so you can see how beautifully it can and has been done. The Where to Find section at the back of the book will help you hunt out details that make all the difference. In addition, each chapter is packed full of exquisite and inspirational photos, which will help you to envisage just how truly wonderful and memorable your vintage wedding day can be.

Will You Marry Me?

Those inimitable and glorious words – so what to do now? When I was asked that magnificent question it was done without the grand presentation of a ring. My lovely husband, as he is now, would probably describe me as exacting, but who isn't when it comes to their wedding day? He explained that he didn't want to choose the wrong ring so offered me a trip into town instead. My first thought of course was vintage! We were on holiday in The Cotswolds when he proposed and so we hurried to the nearest picture-book village to hunt down an antique shop full of hidden gems. Should it take hours to choose an engagement ring? Well it didn't! It took about 15 minutes and I was in love all over again – only this time with a 1920s diamond, white gold and marcasite jewel – and so my vintage wedding love affair began.

← *This perfect combination of pretty tablecloths, glassware, pressed vases and crockery is a total departure from the matching formality of a modern wedding. This mismatched decoration immediately feels intimate and personal.*

↓ *Macaroons stacked in vintage teacups creates a visual feast that looks too good to eat.*

What Makes Your Heart Sing?

In my humble, bridal experience the problem with this vintage wedding business is actually visualizing how it's all going to look. After all, I imagine you're hoping for chic, stylish and charming rather than village hall jumble-sale muddle. Incidentally, I quite like a bit of jumble-sale muddle, but it has its limits. You may be in love with seamed stockings or peonies in teapots, but making it all work together can seem a daunting task and hard to implement from scratch. I remember having a million isolated ideas about little details, such as the colour of the ribbon tied around our napkins or the shade of the tea roses filling little ceramic ink pots, but I had trouble seeing the whole, glorious picture. Where to begin I hear you cry in despair? Unsurprisingly, the best place to start is with *you*. This is what is meant by the old adage, 'it's your day', but it truly is and you need to put your fingerprints all over it! What makes you feel special, go goose-pimply, makes your heart skip a beat? Is it a piece of music, a ravishing pair of shoes, a vase of hand-picked wild flowers, or a jar of buttons? Well then of course all of these things need to be included somehow. So make a list. And if the start of your list includes the word *vintage* then this book is clearly for you!

You may have a loose idea of what you want and perhaps a stronger idea of what you don't – this is good. We all know *that* wedding (the one out of the textbook) – strange, exotic-looking flower arrangements, chairs tied with blousey silk sashes (probably in purple or lime green!), uninspiring white crockery and an off-the-peg dress you've seen before somewhere. A textbook wedding is the exact opposite to the elegance and individuality of a vintage affair. I hope this book will inspire you with ideas and details that will enable you to create a beautiful and, above all, *personal* vintage-inspired wedding that will be the talk of the town for years to come.

Why Vintage?

What is it about vintage that has captured our imaginations, particularly with regard to wedding celebrations? Recycling perhaps or frugality? These factors may play a part, but I'm not sure it is for selfless and practical reasons alone that we long for glorious vintage afternoon tea parties or wonderful antique dresses. I like the idea that every vintage item has its own secret history: perhaps a wedding dress that was worn post-war, or a tiered cake stand used in the 1920s for high tea. This notion weaves in beautifully with the fact that a wedding ceremony is to celebrate the longevity of a relationship. Weddings are about the passage of time and the commitment of years together. How charming and romantic it is to enter into this treaty surrounded by beautiful things that have endured the years, only to settle at your wedding breakfast.

Of course I am overlooking one simple and important aspect to a vintage-inspired extravaganza and that is its beauty. White crockery may be elegant and simple, but it has no flair or personality. Informal flower arrangements spilling over pretty, mismatched china jugs are effortlessly stylish, unlike a formal and restrained bouquet. Vintage can mean simplicity or opulence but it never means dull or mundane.

So, on to the challenge of sourcing those unforgettable pieces that will set you apart from every other bride. Within this book you will discover visual inspiration and a host of advice from specialists. There are also anecdotes about the journey of unearthing the right dress, shoes, jewellery and so on, through personal experience. At the end of the book in the Where to Find section there is a list of where you might find what you're looking for. This list is merely a catalogue of suggestions and you may find many other suppliers that suit your taste and budget. However, these are what I consider to be the most remarkable and stylish of the bunch.

↑ *A stunning 1950s floor-length dress from The Vintage Deli, shown here with leaf earrings by Eclectic Eccentricity and bouquet by Love Blooms.*

THE DRESS

ONE of the potential pitfalls of wearing vintage clothing is the possibility that you end up looking as though you're going to a fancy dress party! Something you definitely want to avoid on such an auspicious occasion. If you choose to wear a 1940s dress it might be advisable to avoid 1940s hair, make-up, shoes, veil and jewellery to match. It is much more visually appealing and personal to choose pieces that you love and then carefully construct a look that is timeless. Both contemporary and vintage can work in perfect balance when handled with care. You can see examples in our photographs of 1940s dresses worn with 1970s shoes or contemporary long, natural hair adorned with a 1940s headpiece and 1920s jewellery. What I'm trying to say is the more you become a slave to one particular period, the less of your own personality you tend to display, so anything goes. This is about beautiful things rather than just vintage things!

➤ *This incredible 1970s scalloped-necked lace dress is set off to perfection with a 1950s waist length veil and needs little extra adornment. In this case, the addition of a diamanté bow choker adds vintage glamour. This style is reminiscent of icons such as Audrey Hepburn and Grace Kelly.*

Finding 'The One'

Now this all sounds perfect in theory, but we're not all fashion stylists and it can be a little frightening choosing clothes and accessories that haven't been endorsed by the stamp of a high street brand or glamorous shop. I often leave second-hand clothes shops empty-handed after struggling with the dilemma, 'does this dress predominantly say Chloe Sevigny or is it a touch more Eliza Doolittle from *My Fair Lady*?'

The wonderful thing about your wedding day is that you tend to have lots of time to plan, so get stuck in as early as possible. I suggest arming yourself with an honest and straight-talking friend who knows your style. Be brave – try it all on. Vintage wedding dresses can often look a little uninspiring when hung limply on a rail, but can have wonderful detailing and fall beautifully. They can also be fitted on you like a glove by a clever seamstress, so even an ill-fitting dress can be nipped and tucked to perfection.

Alternatively, you may have chosen a contemporary dress but are looking for vintage accessories. Just one piece of jewellery or head decoration can be transformational but it's all about finding the perfect item, so try things you wouldn't normally. Who knows if a veil will be the perfect addition to your ensemble? The likelihood is that you've never draped a piece of lace over your face before, and not many of us are accustomed to sporting a pillbox hat or a Juliet cap.

↓ *This 1960s pale cream chiffon dress with covered buttons and three-quarter length sleeves works beautifully with minimal decoration. Softly curled hair and 1950s cutwork peep-toe cream shoes complete this elegant, understated style.*

VARIOUS DRESS STYLES

There are a plethora of dress styles to choose from: the images and descriptions below will give you an idea of the styles to expect from the 1920s through to the 1960s.

← *This Flapper-style wedding dress was typical of the 1920s. Hemlines were shorter than previously seen and fabrics were lightweight and decadent, such as silks, satin and lace. The Juliet cap was popular, often worn with a long veil.*

← *The 1940s wedding silhouette was sleek and slim-lined. Rayon was the popular fabric choice due to the rationing of silk. Full length, long-sleeved gowns were popular, with hand beading, buttoning and lace. Wax crowns with veils attached were favoured.*

← *This classic 1950s wedding look is the perfect combination of a full tulle skirt with a tightly cinched-in waist and cropped veil. Sleeves were often worn long or three-quarter length, as shown here.*

← *Here we can see a return to the floor-length gown although a mini-skirted wedding dress was a popular choice too in the 1960s. A-line skirts and empire lines were favoured for the longer length dresses.*

Where to Begin?

Choosing a vintage wedding dress doesn't necessarily mean an inexpensive alternative, but it certainly does mean unique. The difficulty is where to start and, perhaps more importantly, where to stop. Trying on wedding dresses, whether new or old, feels so exhilaratingly self-indulgent that it's easy to get carried away. My first experience was a modern bridal shop that boasted some vintage-inspired dresses. Pretty much all of it was actually uninspiring, which felt like a huge relief. I had a horrible feeling I was going to fall in love with 30 dresses instantaneously and have a nervous breakdown trying to decide on the right one. I needn't have worried so much! This convinced me that I really wanted my dress to be genuinely old, rather than a modern take on a vintage style.

The first place I came across was The Vintage Wedding Dress Company, which is now known as Charlie Brear, a celebrated treasure trove of vintage finery. There is something indescribable about the feel of an original dress – and they had a selection that set my heart aflutter. I was given an hour to try on as many dresses as I liked in a cocoon-like room of vintage beauty. There was an assistant on hand to discuss possible alterations or additions to any of the dresses if it seemed appropriate and the whole experience was exhilarating and nerve-racking all at the same time. I didn't want to make the wrong decision and felt I had to make a second trip to be sure. After much soul searching, train travel, budget checking and squeezing into various examples of flattering and unflattering regalia, I bought my wedding dress with Charlie Brear and felt marvellously special in it. However, this is one of the higher end boutiques so prices are often not for the faint-hearted, but what you get with Charlie Brear is something

Dress Alterations

exquisite and in immaculate condition, which can be a hard combination to crack on your own.

There are less expensive options if you want the real thing but you may have to work harder to find 'that dress', and it's very likely to require some nimble seamstress fingers to work their magic for you. There are now a plethora of sharp-eyed shopkeepers stocking vintage finery, which wasn't the case when I got married, and so you have a very good chance of tracking down an absolute gem.

The Where to Find section at the back of the book gives a good slice of excellent companies worth looking at and some true experts in their field. This list is certainly not exhaustive, but these are places that I believe offer the very best in vintage wedding dresses at the moment. Of course there are new and exciting companies popping up all the time.

Post purchase, my dress was expertly handled by a company called Bridal Alterations and was transformed from a fairly plain, roomy 1950s dress to a slim-fitting sheath dress with a 1960s lace jacket and a silk tie at the waist, which fell into a loose, soft bow at the back. My dress needed some vision as in its original state it wasn't hugely exciting, but with the help of sound advice I could see what it would become.

A nip and tuck or two is a fairly likely outcome for a vintage wedding dress purchase, so do make sure having staked your claim that you source a seamstress who can handle it with skill and care. There are a number of excellent alterations companies listed in the Where to Find section and there is also an interview with Abigail from Abigail's Vintage Bridal. Abigail not only sells highly desirable, original vintage wedding dresses but also does expert alterations on them, and occasionally on heirloom pieces. She really knows her vintage facts. In the interview she gives some invaluable advice on buying and subsequently having your dress altered.

← This off-the-shoulder lace dress looks absolutely perfect with no additional jewellery. From the wedding of Sophie and Carl Singleton, Standon Hall, Stafford.

→ This 1970s lace dress has covered button detailing and a short net train, topped with a fabric bow at the waist.

ABIGAIL'S VINTAGE BRIDAL

Abigail Haughton worked in costume for film, television and theatre and then moved on to working for a top designer of ladies' evening and bridal wear as a beading designer and quality controller. She now runs Abigail's Vintage Bridal, which offers a comprehensive service selling, altering and fitting your vintage wedding dress. She offers dresses ranging from the turn of the century up until the early 1970s.

. . . .

What are the most common problems that arise when altering a vintage wedding dress?

They tend to be very small — a 66cm (26in) waist can be the norm. Also, working with delicate fabrics can be challenging as dresses have often been stored for long periods and have become fragile. Trying to find colour matches for original fabric can be impossible so I try and work within the parameters of the dress.

Should the bride decide on the underwear they'll be wearing before you begin alterations?

Yes, vintage dresses were often made to be worn over quite supportive undergarments, although this is obviously era dependent. For a seamstress to do an accurate job it is important that the underwear is well fitted and appropriate.

How many times do you usually need to see a bride for a fitting before a dress is complete?

Usually between one and three, depending on the extent of the alterations required. Primary consultations should be six months to a year in advance, with final alterations about a month before the wedding.

◇

Is it possible to repair damaged lace or net, or does it have to be removed if torn or stained?

It is possible to repair but needs to be assessed carefully by a professional. If a dress has significant problems with lace or net it is worth seeking advice in advance of purchasing.

Can a dress be increased in size or lengthened?

A dress can be increased in size. Most vintage dresses are not museum pieces and sometimes require tweaking to bring them into line with more modern sizing and taste, without taking away from the essential style of the original. Vintage dresses tend to be on the smaller side. Significant remodelling can be achieved, altering a dress from a UK size 10 to a 14 for example, but it is dependent on the dress. This is much more costly than hemming and strap alterations. Lengthening a dress can only be achieved on rare occasions. Again, check before purchasing.

Which era offers the most flexibility in terms of alterations?

The 1950s dresses are more flexible because they were often panelled and thus have more fabric in them.

Do some eras work better than others on particular body types, or can most dresses be altered to fit any body shape?

Dresses from the 1950s tend to suit a curvy figure because they are often fitted through the bodice and then flare out to a full skirt, which is more forgiving. Dresses from the 1930s tend to be very figure-hugging and so work wonderfully on more boyish frames. This is obviously a very loose rule of thumb.

Do you have any general advice on choosing the right vintage wedding dress?

Try lots on! The more you try the more you will understand what suits you and you may be surprised. Be flexible with your ideas and do not expect pristine, modern factory finishes.

How much does it cost to have a vintage wedding dress altered?

The cost can be anywhere between £50 and £500.

Body Shape

A friend remarked to me that if she were planning to wear an antique dress at her wedding, she would want some advice on the type of vintage style to suit her body shape. It struck me that women can have very little confidence in their ability to choose clothes to suit their shape, particularly when it comes to something that is out of their general daily wardrobe remit.

However, when it comes to vintage wedding dresses there is no way of knowing what works and what doesn't until you try. It is such an unfamiliar item that I don't think normal rules apply. I remember trying on a selection of dresses, from understated to over-the-top, and was often amazed by the results. One dress looked very figure-hugging on the peg and I'd just had my second baby so wasn't feeling great about my body. When I begrudgingly wiggled into it, I was surprised that the thick, beaded fabric held me in amazingly and I felt incredible in it. It made me realize that wedding dresses are a different beast entirely, particularly vintage pieces because they are such an unknown quantity. Naturally, we all have our body woes and trying a sleeveless dress if you hate your arms is a bit pointless, as is squeezing into a 1920s bias-cut silk number if you're feeling lumpy. Just don't be put off by the so-called rules and you may be pleasantly surprised.

If you do plan on a vintage dress it might be worth sourcing a seamstress before you start and, if you can, taking her with you to the changing room. She will be able to tell you what is possible before you part with your money. I made the mistake of buying two gorgeous vintage wedding dresses from a second-hand clothes shops (thankfully quite cheaply). Both were ridiculously small but I was sure something could be done with them, or rather, with me. Not so! I gazed at them longingly for months until it dawned on me that I was never going to be a size 8, no matter how much altering and abstinence took place. So be realistic about your dress. It might look like 'the one', but if it doesn't fasten up and you're already feeling pretty svelte, or have no desire to give up butter, cheese or chocolate cake, then it probably never will.

Finding a Vintage Treasure

There are a number of online shops that sell vintage dresses, but check carefully that you are allowed to return items that are unsuitable. A dress shipped from afar could be the answer to all your prayers, or a costly mistake when money is of paramount importance. Do remember that many vintage

→ Full-length silk dress with bow detail, from Hope and Harlequin.

↑ *A stunning 1970s cream lace ankle-length high-necked dress accessorized with pale pink ribbon belt and 1970s Cover Girl peep-toe shoes.*

clothes shops don't have all their dresses on display and this is even more likely with wedding dresses. They are often long and incorporate delicate net, lace and silk and so are incredibly hard to display without risk of damage. In your town there are probably a good handful of such shops and some are very likely to have wedding dresses tucked away, so do make sure you ask around. There was one lovely little shop in my local area and the owner had over 20 vintage wedding dresses in a store cupboard, which had never been on display. This is the same for jewellery, shoes, hats, gloves and any other vintage accessories that you might be attempting to track down. Also, don't be afraid to tell anyone who will listen of your plan, as the most unlikely friend or relative may have a hidden gem tucked away gathering dust in their attic.

Shops such as Prim Vintage have the most beautiful selection of original wedding dresses and also have fantastic vintage shoes and accessories, as do The Vintage Deli. The great thing about shops and websites like these is that they don't just cater for brides. You can find wonderful, original bridesmaid dresses, men's clothes and accessories too.

Another way to track down a vintage treasure is to drop into every antique fair you can. There will often be all sorts of exciting things on offer. There are also an ever-growing number of vintage wedding fairs and these will give you an opportunity to hone your vintage hunting skills under one useful roof. These fairs enable you to feel and examine what is on offer. Sometimes a beautiful website with slick photography can belie the true nature of the stock, and on the flip side a most uninspiring website with drab photography can house a dazzling selection of wedding garb. These fairs are a way to ascertain the quality and range on offer. I recommend A Most Curious Wedding Fair as a fantastic resource, and also the Miss Vintage Wedding Affair. However, there are many more fairs throughout the country and there is sure to be one not far from your doorstep.

Vintage-inspired Dresses

You may choose to embark on the arduous but rewarding task of finding your own original vintage dress, but you could opt for a replica dress that would deceive even the most dedicated expert. For example, American company, Twigs and Honey, produces such beautiful dresses it makes me want to get married again! Circa Vintage Brides, Halfpenny London, Juliet Poyser and Claire Pettibone also have breathtaking collections of new dresses. These ranges incorporate vintage silhouettes and detailing that allow them to fall effortlessly between the modern and vintage sphere. They eliminate the problems of aging fabrics, smell, staining and general wear, but offer a pristine alternative with all those longed-for components of a true vintage dress. There are a number of bridal companies that having solely stocked vintage dresses have then gone on to design their own ranges using original designs as inspiration.

➤ *1980s lace dress accessorized with pearl costume jewellery and Kurt Geiger silver shoes. Finished with a 1940s net and bow birdcage veil.*

How to...

WASH A VINTAGE DRESS

It is possible to wash a vintage dress – just take it slowly and carefully, following the basic steps outlined here. Rust can occur from metal clasps or from metal-backed covered buttons, so these need to be removed until the dress has been washed.

1. Submerge the item in lukewarm water – in the bath is ideal. Line the bath with a white sheet first so that when you move the fabric around in the water you agitate the sheet rather than the garment. A wedding dress will become extremely heavy when wet so this sheet will make removing it safer and easier, preventing strain on the fabric or seams. Use a gentle liquid-based detergent, such as Woolite, and leave the dress to soak for up to 36 hours. You can change the water if necessary during this time.

2. Once the garment is rinsed carefully in plenty of fresh water and ready to be removed it must be dried flat. Avoid laying it on wood as this can stain; use a plastic or metal-coated clothing rail. Don't hang the dress up to dry as this will put strain on the delicate old fabric and lace.

3. Once the dress is dry, press it carefully and methodically. It is best to leave the dress very slightly damp as this will help to remove stubborn creases. Start the iron on a low heat (one used for synthetic fibres), and increase the heat gradually. Be on your guard for any sticking, as this means your temperature is too high and you might damage the fabric. Your dress may have many layers and various fabrics so iron each layer one at a time. You can then assess the temperature required and make sure each layer is perfect before moving on.

4. Replace the buttons or metal clasps carefully (or find a seamstress to do it for you) and hopefully, with a little bit of luck, you will have a beautiful stain-free vintage wedding dress.

↑ *Selection of vintage dresses from Hope and Harlequin.*

Made-to-order Dresses

Having a dress made to order means the opportunity to form a relationship with your seamstress and really get to discuss the aspects you wish to incorporate. It helps to have a fairly good idea of the direction you would like your design to take. Your seamstress will then be able to discuss all the possibilities with you and also what sort of vintage shapes will suit your body type. If you need convincing of the outstanding results of a bespoke wedding dress, look no further than Zoe Lem (see the Where to Find section).

Solving Dress Problems

Let's hope that if you've found your dress at an established purveyor of vintage wedding dresses that it will be in excellent condition with no need for mending or stain removal. This isn't to say that it will necessarily fit off the rail. Female body shapes have changed enormously in the last 80 years and we are much taller and larger than our historical counterparts. This can make it difficult to find dresses that are instantly wearable. Again, this is where the invaluable seamstress comes in and there are clever tricks to lengthen, take in, let

← *1960s full-length chiffon white dress with full sleeves and train. This needs little embellishment and is set off perfectly with a single peony bloom in the bride's hair.*

plumping for a dress. A strategically placed corsage or ribbon can disguise a tiny fault but if half the bodice of your dress has distinctive marks or staining then it's important to be realistic about the possible outcome of unstitching or trying to de-stain your dress.

Odour

This is a tricky problem to deal with without washing. If the dress is stained too then you will be tackling the odour issue when you wash it or when you have it professionally cleaned. However, if the dress is in perfect condition and doesn't need cleaning but has a musty smell then the best solution is to air it. Hang it in the garden and give it a good breath of fresh air for as long as possible. Cover it to protect against birds.

Stain and Discolouration Removal

Staining or discolouration is one of the most likely problems to befall a vintage item and of course a wedding dress or veil fabric is liable to be delicate. Dresses are often constructed of silk, lace or net and sometimes a combination of all three, which are notoriously difficult to work with in terms of stain removal. Your dress may have spot stains, rust stains from metal clasps or even be completely discoloured throughout. However, do not despair just yet. If you are nervous of attempting a DIY job, thankfully there are experts that will do this for you. Some deal specifically with vintage clothing and I have listed two of the best in the Where to Find section. The reality is if they can't remove an unsightly stain, then you may have to resign yourself to your vintage find being a lost cause. Alternatively, if you are feeling brave and thrifty there are ways to try and revive your dress using a few simple techniques – see How to Wash a Vintage Dress (previously described).

out and embellish a dress to make it look as good as new, but still retain its wonderful authenticity.

Alternatively, you may have found your dream dress in a charity shop or an antique fair where the items may not be in such fabulous condition. As with anything kept in the cupboard or attic for years there are a million possible problems arising from storage, such as moth holes, staining, rips, fading and even just smelling a bit odd! It's imperative to have a good idea of the solutions to these problems before

An interview with...

HOPE AND HARLEQUIN

Louise Hill runs Hope and Harlequin in Brighton, selling beautiful, original vintage wedding dresses and accessories. Louise gained a Fine Art Degree in London and then worked for Sarah Arnett Bride on made-to-order wedding dresses. She has always favoured vintage clothing, preferring it to the constant merry-go-round of mainstream fashion. There is longevity and heritage to vintage, which makes it infinitely more appealing. This interest, coupled with her experience in the wedding industry, inspired her to set up Hope and Harlequin.

What would you say are the potential problems with choosing a vintage dress?

Size alteration can sometimes be tricky. Also, damage and the luck of finding something that you actually love and feel great in, without looking as if you have stepped out of a bygone era! Basically, you don't want your wedding dress to look like a costume. A dress really has to suit a personality and should not wear the bride. As long as the dress is alterable then size can be dealt with, but it needs to have someone sympathetic to the authenticity of the garment to work with it, as otherwise it can look a bit cobbled together. I encourage clients not to add too many modern details or to change the original a huge amount as I think it detracts from the point of the piece. We offer a made-to-order service if a client would like an alternative to an original dress, which grew out of a need to offer a choice of style, quality, fit and new fabric, but using vintage shapes so the dress has the soul of an earlier piece. We also offer 'peace silks' as a way of minimizing the environmental impact of our dresses. The standard procedure for producing silk is to boil whole cocoons, which are later unravelled onto reels into a single silk strand. This process kills the silkworm inside. Peace silk uses a different procedure. Instead of being reeled, the silk undergoes a process of degumming and is then spun in a similar manner as other fibres. This means that the silkworm is allowed to live out its full life-cycle but still produces lovely silk yarn.

How many vintage dresses do you tend to have in stock at any one time?

We usually have between 10 and 30 vintage wedding dresses available.

What specific services do you offer your vintage wedding dress customers?

We sell online but also offer one-to-one appointments at the shop in a specific boutique. We also offer advice on alteration possibilities and have a brilliant seamstress who will do this work. We mend and alter dresses usually after a purchase has been made. Dresses are dry-cleaned and altered to hide any stains or wear and tear.

Is there an era that is particularly popular at the moment?

The 1930s are always popular as it was such a glamorous time. The 1960s also seem to be coming into fashion again, probably due to mainstream fashion influence.

What do you think is the attraction of buying vintage?

Originality, heritage and sometimes also cost, but mainly the feeling of having something unique that has been loved and worn by someone else. Originality is something that is hard to find today, and I think this appeals to women when buying vintage. You are claiming a little piece of history every time an old dress is worn for a new ceremony. It is a return to more traditional values of wearing one's best for a wedding rather than having something totally new. It suits the cultural shift towards 'make do and mend'. There is also a huge amount of work in a vintage dress, which is not often matched by its modern counterpart. Handmade lace is practically a lost art these days, without it costing a fortune, so it is a chance to have something that has had skill and time spent on it that most of us simply cannot afford. The fabrics are fantastic and, again, are not matched by modern alternatives, unless you can afford couture! The environmental aspect of sustainability is an added bonus.

THE LINGERIE

IT goes without saying that what you wear under your dress is virtually as important as the dress itself. Perhaps words like 'scaffolding' and 'structure' ought to be bandied around as much as 'luxurious' and 'romantic'. With regard to wedding underwear, form and function are both of paramount importance. At some point all will be revealed and so it must be exquisitely tantalizing and also work its technical magic at the same time. This is even more imperative if your dress is vintage, as it will almost certainly be structurally quite different to a modern dress. Upon arriving at my first wedding dress fitting the seamstress exclaimed in horror at the shapeless, unsupportive bra I was sporting and sent me packing with strict instructions to purchase an appropriate undergarment before she would deign to begin! So don't make that same mistake and ensure that you've already sourced your wedding underwear before you commence with dress fittings.

➤ *Replica 1940s underwear set in oyster pink silk.*

Structured Lingerie

In terms of wedding underwear, perhaps opting for something that is vintage-inspired but with modern genius is the key, rather than your grandmother's hand-me-down brassiere. Unless, of course, you find something in beautiful condition that fits like a glove – which isn't beyond the realms of possibility. There are some fabulous websites stocked full of vintage and vintage-inspired hosiery (see Where to Find). This list is by no means exhaustive. There are a multitude of companies to choose from, but these are the ones I feel offer the finest in vintage undergarments, or the most fabulous modern alternatives that look exquisite and are reminiscent of their historical counterparts.

The type of underwear you actually choose will naturally depend heavily on your dress type. Obviously, a 1920s bias-cut clinging silk number will need very careful planning underwear-wise, as a visible panty line is simply not acceptable and a boned corset is likely to look lumpy! Also, you may feel that you would like something supportive and toning, which probably means not so pretty, so do think carefully about what your lingerie will do for the dress as much as what it will do for your new husband. This may well mean seeking professional advice but a number of my suggested stockists are extremely well versed in giving underwear advice. If the worst comes to the worst and you don't want to reveal your support knickers or undress to reveal no bra at all due to strategically placed tape, you can always do a quick change before bedtime!

The first place to mention is a real find and they are absolute aficionados when it comes to vintage underwear. What Katie Did is a Mecca for vintage and vintage-inspired undergarments and they cover everything from cinching-in corsets to provocative and ethereal sheer knickers. They also stock fabulous hosiery so are the perfect place to find those must-have seamed stockings or fishnets. We have an interview with Katie Thomas from What Katie Did at the end of this section, which will hopefully answer many of your underwear queries. A company called Kiss Me Deadly stock incredible corsets, basques, girdles, suspender belts and more. Many of these items are designed to hold you in and look fabulous at the same time, which is obviously the perfect combination for the real woman. Kiss Me Deadly also has lots of very helpful information on their website about measuring yourself and what and why they stock what they do.

← *1950s-style white satin basque.*

↑ *Vintage lace camisole with ribbon straps.*

➤ *1930s silk stockings in original box.*

Unstructured Lingerie

On the other side of the vintage coin is the breathtakingly beautiful range of Claire Pettibone. This is not underwear to hold you in or push you up. These are lace and silk concoctions that evoke romantic interludes and what wedding nights are intended for. On a practical level, and particularly if you're not naturally a size 6 with a washboard stomach and miniscule bottom, it may be something you would choose to change into as your dress may require something a little more robust. LovebySusie cover every angle. They stock waspies and corsets to delight and control, but also divine, floating vintage-inspired French knickers and lace nightdresses too. If you have something very specific in mind there is Stockings and Romance who make bespoke underwear.

So the rule of thumb is find your dress and then think seriously about what you need your underwear to do for you. What you choose will be the difference between looking good and looking downright fabulous. A good bra or a defined waist really does matter and especially so with vintage clothing. In the 1940s or 50s women didn't tend to do loose and floating. Dresses were meant to show off your fabulous figure and the curvier the better, so if you haven't got those curves fake them and if you have, celebrate them with some good support.

Hosiery

Stockings can be a bit of a tricky number as many of us don't really wear them these days. There was a time when a stocking was the only option but tights (pantyhose) are now standard regalia and stockings can seem a little complicated. However, there is also something exciting and of course a little bit risqué about the suspender and stocking paraphernalia, and it is your wedding day. Many of the companies already mentioned have a good selection of stockings and suspender belts and will offer advice. There is also a very clever company called Muuna Hosiery. They don't have a website but will embellish stockings with beautiful beading and embroidery. Details are in the Where to Find section at the back of the book.

An interview with...

KATIE THOMAS AT WHAT KATIE DID

Katie Thomas is the founder of What Katie Did, a vintage lingerie company launched in 1999. She is an expert on 1940s and 1950s underwear and has used her expertise to run this hugely successful business for over ten years. Her knowledge and advice will be invaluable to any bride planning to wear vintage lingerie.

Are your underwear designs based on original pieces?

The majority of our designs are inspired by vintage pieces, although this varies greatly depending on the piece. For example, our Maitresse bullet bra, CC09 French knickers and CC09 bra are almost identical to styles worn in the 1940s and 1950s. Our underwired bras tend to include vintage detailing but are cut to a more modern shape, as underwired bras were in their infancy in the 1950s and didn't offer the support or fit that women expect today.

◆

Do you have anywhere I can come and try lingerie on?

We have two boutiques, one on Portobello Road in West London and one on Melrose Avenue in Hollywood, California. We also supply numerous stores – a full list of stockists can be found on our website.

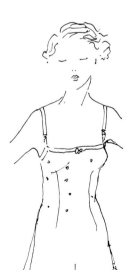

◆

Do you offer a complete measuring service?

We offer an expert measuring service in our stores, and a virtual sizing service online.

◆

What sizes do you cater for?

Our sizes run from UK size 8 to 18 and cup sizes A to G.

Can you explain the difference between a basque, a corset and a girdle?

A corset is the most serious piece of shapewear and is made from non-stretch fabric, should be fully steel-boned and have laces at the back, which you pull to cinch in your waist to the desired size. A girdle is made of stretch fabric that gently shapes the body, smoothing out lumps and bumps. Whilst a girdle won't dramatically alter the figure like a corset, it is extremely comfortable and requires no practise to wear. A girdle is mainly designed to shape the hips and bottom but there are other options, such as a corselette, which includes a bra and so shapes the whole torso resulting in an extremely smooth line. Basques in general aren't designed to shape the body, but offer support to the bust and look very alluring! At What Katie Did we don't offer a traditional basque, as we like our lingerie to earn its keep. Instead we offer a 1950s Merry Widow, a forerunner of the basque that incorporates a waist cincher and a torsolette, which is a strapless corselette gently shaping the whole torso.

Can you help me choose the right piece to go under my wedding dress and if so do I need to bring it with me to an underwear fitting?

Fitting brides-to-be is one of our favourite things to do and yes, it helps greatly if they bring their dress. Brides often think they know what shapewear they need but it turns out they need something entirely different. It's always best to book an appointment with us so that we can reserve our private fitting area where brides (and bridesmaids/mothers) can relax and have room to move around, sit, bend, stretch and dance to ensure that they're truly comfortable and that everything stays exactly where it should.

Will a suspender belt be visible under a fitted dress?

This is often a concern, but unless the dress is a close-fitting, bias-cut thin silk or satin dress, suspender bumps won't show.

Are specific types of underwear better suited to particularly shaped dresses?

Yes – it all depends on the shape of the dress. A close-fitting dress will require a torsolette or corselette to give a smooth line, flattening the tummy and smoothing the hips. A tight-fitting bodice with a full skirt will require a Merry Widow, waist cincher or corset to tightly nip in the waist for an hourglass shape.

THE SHOES

WHEN you don't have to worry about handbags for once, the shoe choice is elevated to near god-like status, and even if your dress is a floor scraper and your show-stopping footwear will only be glimpsed momentarily, this is not a decision to be entered into lightly. Whatever happens regarding your shoes, there is no question that your choice of footwear needs to strike the right chord. You might choose to wear a white tulle 1950s knee length dress and finish it off with an impeccable pair of red stilettos. Alternatively, you may have always longed to wear ballet flats on your wedding day, or sparkling silver platforms. Just make sure that whatever you choose you can walk, stand up, sit down, kneel (if necessary) and dance in them without too much conspicuous discomfort. It is also important to consider your dress choice carefully and decide which is to take centre stage as your statement piece. Do your shoes need to fit around your dress, or should the dress be perfect for the shoes you've fallen for? Heel height is also an important decision and should be considered prior to your dress length being attended to.

➤ *A tempting selection of vintage and contemporary shoes, ranging from the 1920s through to the present day.*

← *1960s black and pink stilettos.*

Original Vintage

The thing about vintage shoes is that they are often on the diminutive side and women today have evolved rather less dainty feet than our historical counterparts. Falling in love with a pair of 1920s flapper girl shoes is a touch deflating when they're a size 3 and you're a size 6! Of course it's not impossible to find something extraordinary and beautiful that fits, but you will have to shop with a surge of dedication and tenacity that you never thought possible. The other slight downside with a vintage shoe is their general wear and tear. It makes the search doubly hard when that perfect vintage shoe needs to be in immaculate condition and marvellously comfortable too. However, it is not impossible that you could be blessed with a minor miracle in a vintage clothing store and experience a real life 'glass slipper' moment.

Vintage-inspired Footwear

If the glass slipper moment eludes you there is a plethora of ravishing vintage-style footwear around these days, which would fool even a Biba expert. One such brilliant example is the US-based store, Remix Shoes. This company have a wide range of stunning vintage-inspired shoes for men and women. Shoe designers such as Rachel Simpson, Harriet Wilde and Diane Hassall all produce exquisite wedding footwear and the high street boasts an overwhelming amount of delicious shoes too, so your ideal choice will be out there somewhere in one form or another. Also, as I've hinted at before, it can potentially be a mistake to be slavishly tied to the vintage look from head to toe. Not a girl in the world can argue with a pair of this season Manolo Blaniks to catapult that 1950s frock into the style stratosphere!

Dyeing Shoes

So apart from tracking down that vintage heart stopper, or buying something new and heavenly there are a couple of other options up your sleeve. You could dye a pair of shoes yourself. This opens up a million possibilities, but is not for the faint-hearted – I have outlined opposite how to dye a pair of shoes if you're feeling brave. On the plus side there are companies that will dye your shoes for you, for example, Girls of Elegance offer a full shoe dyeing service.

↓ *Modern bottle green suede shoes by Ravel.*

How to...

DYE A PAIR OF SHOES

If you're attempting to dye a natural fabric, such as silk, cotton or linen, you will need to use a dye suitable for natural fibres. If the shoes are a synthetic material, such as polyester, then the dye must be appropriate for man-made fibres. You will certainly need to practise the dyeing technique and check colour swatches before you wield your paintbrush aloft.

1. Once you have selected the correct dye type for your shoe fabric, mix the dye according to the packet instructions. Add more water for a less intense colour.

2. Fill the shoes with white kitchen/tissue paper to prevent dye from seeping in to the inside of the shoes.

3. Use a good quality wide, flat paintbrush to paint on the shoe dye, using long, smooth strokes to ensure that the dye is painted on evenly. The secret is to layer up the dye, so paint two coats, allow to dry and then repeat with another two coats. Continue until you are happy with the depth of colour and then allow the shoes to air dry.

↑ *From the wedding of Joanna and Dave Adkins, London.*

Shoe Decorations

There is an endless and exciting parade of shoe clips, ribbons, bows and jewels to transform pedestrian court shoes into the eighth wonder of the world. Have a look at Absolutely Audrey, an American company with a fabulous selection of new and vintage shoe clips. This is the perfect way to embellish shoes without having to make any permanent changes. At the other end of the scale look at My Glass Slipper: they have a choice of plain shoes available and you can select from a wide range of decorations, which they will attach to your shoes. Nicky Rox will decorate any pair of shoes with anything your heart desires and she even runs shoe decorating workshops. This enables you to unleash your inner shoe designer under the watchful eye of an experienced professional.

Shoe clips are particularly appealing as they are removable so you can't make a long-term mistake. Incidentally, shoe clips are a charming addition to the shoes for your bridesmaids

and flower girls too. Little ballet shoes with pretty butterfly clips or sequins can look enchanting.

If you want something completely bespoke but are too nervous to attempt the decoration yourself then look no further than two amazing companies – Figgie Shoes and Hetty Rose. These companies will embellish and personalize your shoes to within an inch of their lives and the results are quite simply brilliant. Deborah Thompson at the American company Figgie Shoes will literally hand paint your shoes with details that reflect exactly who you are. You talk to Figgie Shoes about places and people that are important to you and everything can be incorporated into your decorative shoe design. You buy the shoes and Figgie Shoes does the rest!

Alternatively, and equally as captivating are the shoes of UK-based Hetty Rose Limited. Henrietta will work closely with you to decorate and design your shoes using vintage

↑ *Shoes from the wedding of Kate and Rod Beer, Dorking.*

← *The prettiest pink peep-toe shoes and little ballet pumps. From the wedding of Kelly and James Alcock, Braziers Park, Reading.*

finds to reflect your personality and taste. She particularly favours using vintage Japanese kimono fabrics and she has kindly given an interview to answer your questions about using a bespoke shoe-designing service.

Design Your Own Shoes

There is one alternative that looks like great fun, and that is to design your own shoes! There are companies, such as Shoes of Prey or Emmy Shoes, that will work with you to create the shoe of your dreams. You can incorporate every little vintage nuance or twist that takes your fancy, but also consider all the elements that make up your perfect shoe. For example, perhaps you have seen your dream shoe but the heel is too high. You can ensure a beautiful result that is visually spectacular and comfortable too. Although to be perfectly honest you may not notice a pair of crippling shoes when you're walking on cloud nine. I didn't realize until post-wedding that I had endured an uncomfortable right shoe and sported a black toenail for a year after my wedding – an unsightly keepsake to say the least!

An interview with...

HETTY ROSE LIMITED

Henrietta Rose Samuels graduated from the London College of Fashion with a degree in Footwear Design and Development and then worked in London and Italy for handmade shoe companies. She set up her company Hetty Rose in 2007 and was selected to exhibit at London Fashion Week in her first season. She now features at many shows and exhibitions and hosts shoe parties too.

When did you start designing shoes?

My mother said on my very first day of nursery school she asked me what my teacher was like and all I talked about were her shiny red shoes! So I knew from an early age I was very taken with footwear. Following my childhood obsession, I went on to spend four years studying Footwear Design and Development at Cordwainers (London College of Fashion). I worked for other designers after graduating but knew I wanted my name inside the shoe. I set up the Hetty Rose brand in 2007, which is an ethical, handmade shoe company based on a theory of re-using and re-working vintage materials in a creative and sustainable way, hand making shoes to fit.

Can customers bring shoes to you that they've already chosen or do you always design the shoe from scratch?

I design a collection for clients to choose from, although they can change the heels or colours, and we can even create a completely bespoke design if they have something in mind.

Once I've selected my shoe design what is the next step?

I design and hand make the shoes to order in a workshop in London. You can view the current Kimono Collection online at www.hettyrose.co.uk, choose a style, and have it made to measure and in a vintage kimono fabric. As I hand make the shoes we can design the perfect shoes for you, and you can choose from lots of heels, colours and fittings.

How much choice is there in terms of the fabric available?

I have a good stock of kimono fabric, and my contacts in Japan can send me options if a client is looking for something specific.

You favour using Japanese vintage Kimono fabric, but do you offer other design options?

I primarily up-cycle vintage Japanese kimono fabrics, each holding different meanings shown by their use of colour and graphics. Using such interesting materials means these shoes go deeper than aesthetic glamour. The kimono fabrics from Japan have stories behind them and the colours and designs have different meanings. I love telling clients about the fabric they have chosen for their shoes. They have an emotional attachment to their purchase; it's more of an experience as they are involved in choosing the fabric, the style, the heel and so on. I send them photos as I make their shoes so they can see how they are developing. However, I do offer other options. Some people bring a special fabric to me, or the same fabric or a trimming from their wedding dress. I had a client who had her family tartan woven for her husband-to-be's kilt. We made her shoes from the same fabric and they looked great! I've even covered buttons for the groom in the same fabric as the bride's shoes. As everything is bespoke, I can help with many aspects of the accessories that go alongside the shoes for the big day.

How many fittings are needed, or can you make the shoes without measuring in person?

The process includes taking measurements and photos of the feet and doing a fitting at a halfway stage. I am based in south London and you are welcome to come to the studio. If you live further afield you can still have your dream shoes made. I can explain how to measure your own feet (it's not too difficult!), email/post the information to me here at the workshop and then go from there. I have made shoes for lots of clients all over the world – we do everything over email.

How long does it take for a pair of shoes to be made, and what do they cost?

It takes around eight weeks for the whole process, with lots of drying and moulding in between. Each pair takes about 20 hours spread out over those weeks. The shoes start from £430, which is payable in two deposits.

VEILS AND HEADDRESSES

NO one can dispute how utterly captivating the moment is when the beautiful, partially hidden face of a bride-to-be is revealed, filled with anticipation and trepidation in equal measure. Veils never fail to add that air of suspense and there seems to be an almost infinite selection of styles and fabrics to choose from – everything from floor-sweeping opulence to a sassy little net number. This wide choice means that this can be a difficult decision to make but I give plenty of advice in this chapter. I feel rather wistful about the veil as I secretly wish I had worn one on my wedding day. I felt a bit foolish trying a veil on, but on reflection I regret not persevering – so take heed and be brave. This is your one and only chance to embrace so much beautiful lace and net! I have secretly popped one on during the odd photo shoot, and that tumbling sheer fabric is a joy to behold. I suppose you never really tire of dressing up!

→ *A stunning silk cap with birdcage veil and beading, by Annelli Clarke.*

Traditional Veils

Sweeping veils are back on the wedding map at the moment, which seems an odd thing to say but for a time they were less likely to make an appearance. However, a burgeoning love affair with vintage pieces, plus public weddings featuring stunning veils have put them firmly back in their place.

There are so many styles to choose from (see the Veil Styles feature later in this chapter) and the effect can be stately and imposing or delicately pretty depending on length, cut and ornamentation. Vintage veils can be hard to find in immaculate condition, simply because even when worn once they were so very delicate and liable to get trodden on or torn by enthusiastic well-wishers. A good option here is eBay, as veils are often kept tucked away in attics and lofts. They may require some love and attention but the effect of an original veil can be utterly captivating and there is something so special about wearing a garment with its own history.

Among my favourites are veils from the 1930s and 40s. It was very much in vogue to have a crown or headdress made from wax atop your veil. These are becoming extremely rare and, unfortunately, this is not a skill that we replicate today. Some of these wax flowers and buds were incredibly intricate and delicate and many have been damaged over time. If you do find one in amazing condition you're a lucky girl, so snap it up! Fabric flowers were also a popular addition and again may not always stand the test of time, but these can possibly be removed, replaced or cleaned by a professional.

If you are set on an old veil there are places such as US-based Dolls and Lace and The Vintage Bride, but you have to be quick as these original pieces go very quickly. Veils also pop up in little vintage clothes shops and antique fairs so keep your eyes open. In the UK, Honiton Lace, despite not having an online shop or photographs, has a fantastic array

of antique lace veils and you may just have to take a trip into the beautiful Devon countryside to view them, which doesn't seem like a hardship. Antique Lace Heirlooms is also worth investigating as they too have a marvellous selection.

There are of course companies that make absolutely heavenly new veils based on every possible original style. For example, Unveiled Bridal Designs is a sweetie shop of possibilities, as is LovebySusie. These websites give you very useful information on differing styles, from floor-sweeping cathedral veils to mantillas. Susie McKenzie from LovebySusie also gives great advice about options and styles in her interview later in this section.

Birdcage Veil

If you feel that a traditional lace, cathedral, church or shoulder length veil is just a little too grandiose, there are plenty of other delightful and more modest or striking options for your wedding day – not least of all, the birdcage veil. This clipped veil became popular in the 1930s and 40s and was soon the modern alternative to a traditional fabric veil. Its short net covering frames the face perfectly and can be teamed with almost any piece of hair jewellery, comb or pillbox hat to create a modish and elegant statement. This means that it is unfailingly versatile and if chosen with care can work with virtually any period or modern dress. It also suggests both confidence and poise, which can be a winning combination when you are perhaps feeling a bit of an absence of both. Conceal those butterflies behind a veil or appear to be the epitome of poise and calm in an elegant birdcage veil or pillbox hat.

Veil Alternatives

Pillbox Hat
The pillbox was a firm fixture on the 1930s to 1960s fashion scene and has made a recent reappearance, particularly as a wedding headpiece. The pillbox is usually a circular shape with flat edges (a bit like a small hat box lid), often decorated and sometimes with a short net veil. They can be attached to most hairstyles easily and usually need to be pinned into place as they are normally fairly modest in size. A common fabric used for this type of hat is felt, but silk and straw alternatives can be found. Pillbox hats are particularly appropriate for smart, city weddings. You may choose to combine it with quite a structured dress and often the style of the pillbox works particularly well on 1940s- and 50s-style up-do hairstyles.

← *Silk and sequin 1950s wedding hat.*

← ← *1950s white veil with a fabric flower headdress and diamanté bow choker.*

Lace Headbands

A headband is such a dainty alternative to the traditional veil, particularly if you want to make a slightly less grand statement but with the same startling effect. Indicative of classic ballerinas, the Alice band in its many guises can complete a vintage-style look to perfection. The photographs here depict beautiful chiffon and lace bands, which can be found at an American company called Garlands of Grace. These bands work particularly well with expertly styled up-dos, reminiscent of a prima ballerina, or with the hair down and softly tousled. If this type of headdress appeals I implore you to study their website. Their made-to-order lace bands with ribbon ties are absolutely exquisite.

↓ *White chiffon headband,*
from Garlands of Grace.

↓ *Cream lace headband,*
from Garlands of Grace.

VEIL STYLES

There are many factors to consider in the design of a veil, including length, cut/style, fabric, edging, trim and accents. Here are some descriptions from Susie McKenzie.

Veil Length

Birdcage veil – very short, normally a slightly ruched piece of cage netting or tulle that only covers the face or part of the face/forehead.

Shoulder length, elbow length, waist length – as described.

Fingertip length – a veil that falls to your fingertips when your arms lie straight along your sides.

Waltz length – length falls between your knees and ankles, allowing you to dance with ease.

Chapel length – a very romantic and popular length that reaches to the floor and extends about a metre/yard past your hem.

Cathedral length – can be exceptionally long extending for metres – long aisle required!

Veil Cut

Standard cut – initially a rectangular shape with the bottom corners rounded off so that the edges of the veil start by your face. Normally the top of the fabric is gathered at a comb to create a volume of varying degrees.

Angel or cascade cut – the sides start higher on the side of the veil, 'cascading' down.

Circular cut – basically a circle folded in half to create two tiers (blusher). This can be gathered at the fold and sewn to a comb. The edges of the veil are down at the bottom, not up by the face.

Oval cut/mantilla veil – a one-tier veil without blusher that is cut in the shape of an oval and worn normally flat to the head with no gathers. A mantilla veil will have a beautiful lace edge all around.

Veil Fabric

Tulle is the standard veil fabric but there are different types depending on the look you want.

Soft silk tulle – 100% silk, very soft luxury tulle and so delicate, creating a beautifully flowing, light as air veil, which drapes beautifully down the body.

Silk veiling tulle – 84% silk/16% polyamide, very luxurious but has a crispness to it that can create more shape rather than flow.

Synthetic tulle/bridal illusion – most commonly used in 100% nylon and is diamond-shaped interlock fabric. Excellent for use in a veil with blusher as its crispness gives high pouf when gathered.

English tulle – English netting made from 100% cotton with a hexagonal interlock. It is heavier and stiffer than other tulles.

Cage net – type of stiff netting generally only used for birdcage veils and hats.

Veils can be made from other sheer fabrics, such as organza and chiffon, for a less traditional look.

Special tulles – you can also choose from synthetic and silk tulles with spots/polka dots and tulles with shimmer/glitter all over.

Edging, Trims and Accents

Edges – cut edge (raw edge), pencil edge (a versatile plain finish that can be done very finely by hand or by machine), satin ribbon edge, corded edge or a lace trim edge.

Accents – embellishments scattered over the veil or around the edges or hem only. Can include pearls, crystals and rhinestones.

Fascinators

Fascinators are generally made of feathers, beads and fabric flowers and are usually attached to the side of the head. The base tends to be quite small and is often just a comb or a sizeable clip. This means that it can be easily and firmly fixed in place. This type of decoration has had a huge revival recently and can be adapted to suit any type of occasion.

Flower Crowns

The romantic vision of a fresh flower crown is so evocative of fairy stories and woodland nymphs, what ethereal vintage bride could resist? These beautiful headdresses have had a huge resurgence recently and it's easy to see why as these flower crowns are so suggestive of innocence and enchantment. For inspiration look no further than the flower fairy drawings of Cecily Barker. The fantastic thing about these floral crowns is that they can be as simple as a daisy chain or as flamboyant, colourful and decadent as you like. Either way they never fail to delight. A good florist will be able to make you a wonderful flower crown.

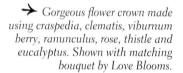

➤ *Gorgeous flower crown made using craspedia, clematis, viburnum berry, ranunculus, rose, thistle and eucalyptus. Shown with matching bouquet by Love Blooms.*

← *Feather fascinator by Annelli Clarke.*

Feather Headdresses

A breathtaking head crown is not for everyone but it certainly makes the most incredible statement. This Indian-style feather headdress, as seen in our photo shoot at Mannington Hall, was made by Annelli Clarke and we were all so excited about it. When twinned with a stunning vintage wedding dress and very little else this really packs a visual punch – definitely not a wall flower look.

Reviving Vintage Veils

Vintage veils can be breathtakingly beautiful but as they are often handed down through the years they can become moth-eaten, discoloured and lacklustre, despite careful storage. Do not despair. If you are intent on breathing life into your great-grandmother's veil this is not impossible, even if it is ailing. It may be worth taking the garment to a professional cleaner and asking for their advice. However, dry-cleaners may use products that are not kind to vintage fabrics so be careful who you choose. Companies such as Mayflower Cleaners have a special service for cleaning vintage clothing. Perry De Montaignac (PDEM) specialize in using gentle and environmentally friendly products to deal with the delicate fabrics of vintage wedding dresses and veils. Antique Lace Heirlooms will not only clean but also repair, re-bead and restore your antique items. The Honiton Lace Shop will also clean your antique veil for you and really know their stuff when it comes to storing and preserving vintage items.

➤ *Pheasant feather headdress with fabric band by Annelli Clarke, worn with a 1970s wedding dress.*

How to...

WASH A VINTAGE VEIL

The following instructions apply to white veils, as bleach is used. If your veil has cream netting then seek professional advice so the veil doesn't get damaged further. Don't use this process if your veil has a wax or beaded headdress, as these could be adversely affected by bleaching. If the item looks very weak in places, or as if it may not survive too much intervention, seek professional advice. It would be terrible to ruin something that really requires expert skill.

1. Sandwich the veil flat between two clean white towels. This will prevent it from being in direct contact with the bleach. Fold in any edges that are larger than the surface area of the towel.

2. Prepare a bath of warm water, adding a bleach and water solution mixed according to the bleach manufacturer's instructions. A good bleach for this process is Clorox 2, which is a powder. Dissolve the bleach in hot water before adding it to the bath tub.

3. Submerge the towel and veil sandwich into the bath. The soaking time can vary: check after 15–20 minutes and keep doing so until about two hours has passed.

4. When you are happy that the colour has changed sufficiently rinse the veil and towels carefully with cold water, still leaving them lying as flat as possible. Remove the towel cover, gently squeeze out excess water and find somewhere to lay the veil completely flat to dry, placing it on a clean white towel.

A stunning veil from the wedding of Chau and Tom Baskaga, Marylebone Town Hall, London.

How to...

DYE A VEIL

You may have found the perfect veil in style but not colour, which isn't necessarily the end of the world. You can age netting or lace beautifully by simply using good old-fashioned tea. There are just two things to remember if you wish to embark on a home dyeing exercise. First, you can't undo a tea dye, so once it's done it's done. Second, as with any dyeing process, natural fibres, such as cotton or silk, are more responsive to colour than artificial ones, so be sure to check your fabric type before you begin.

1. Find a large pan that the veil can move in without getting bunched up or folded (old jam pans are perfect). Fill with water and bring to the boil. Once boiling, add your tea bags and let them sit until the water looks like the right colour for your item. This is hard to judge without doing a trial run, so do some swatch tests to determine how many tea bags will alter the colour to your desired level.

2. When you're happy with the strength of colour in the water remove the pan from the heat and allow the water to cool completely.

3. Rinse the veil in clean, cold water to make it evenly wet. Now add the veil to the tea solution, ensuring that it's not bunched up and is completely submerged. Keep an eye on it to assess the colour change and when you're happy remove it and rinse it in cold, clear water.

4. Find somewhere to hang the item or lay it completely flat so it dries with no creases – over the bath can be a good place.

↑ *The wedding of Hels and Lewis, photographed by Laura Mccluskey Photography.*

An interview with...

LovebySusie

Susie McKenzie established LovebySusie in 2007 following a BA (Hons) degree in Fashion Design, an MSc in Fashion Marketing and a number of years in the fashion industry, gaining knowledge and expertise in all aspects of the design, construction and production of exquisite high quality garments. Susie works from her studio in Edinburgh, but ships internationally. The latest range is bridal accessories – from silk chiffon and tulle veils to vintage lace cover-ups and silk capelets.

Do you have a shop where a customer can come and try on different veil styles?

I don't have a shop but veils will be available for wholesale in 2013 due to interest from UK boutiques. I will also take commissions for custom veils, where brides can try on veils at my studio so we can create a unique veil or headpiece.

◆

Do you think the veil has had a recent resurgence and if so why?

Definitely and it's part of the huge trend for all things vintage-inspired, from couture to ready to wear. This has been accelerated by famous brides Kate Moss, Lily Allen and Kate Middleton, who wore floaty silk and lace-embellished veils and Juliet cap-style lace headpieces. Similar versions of the Juliet Cap can be more like a soft cap or wide band in lace or tulle, which is either part of the veil or a separate piece to be worn on top on its own.

◆

What is your most popular veil or headpiece style at the moment?

The Liliana Lace Juliet Cap is a truly lovely wedding headpiece for a vintage-inspired wedding. In palest ivory or vintage cream, the shaped lace cap is created from floral vintage design Nottingham Cluny lace with beautiful scalloped edges. It is hand beaded with Swarovski crystals or freshwater pearls and finished with hand-cut lace flowers at the sides. The Gwyneth Lace Trim Silk Veil is also popular; an exquisite circular cut veil with blusher in super soft, delicate ivory silk tulle with either cream or pale ivory Nottingham lace trimming. This silk tulle is soft and delicate, floating to the ground and it is available in chapel/floor and waist length.

Any tips for the veil-wearing bride?

Take your hair accessories and veil to your trial wedding hair appointments. If you want to wear a tiara or hairband it's essential that it works with your veil and hair type/style. Consider if you want your veil to be visible in all or some of your photographs, and also if you want your veil to make a statement from front and back views. Try some veils on when trying on gowns as you may be surprised how they can complement and complete a bridal ensemble!

Is it important to have chosen your dress before choosing a veil?

Yes – the dress is normally the starting piece, as you need a style to suit your body shape and many gowns may not suit a veil. The fabric and colour of the veil will also be easier to match to the dress, rather than the other way around.

Should the bride have decided on a hairstyle before embarking on veil choice?

I think they go hand in hand. The fine, floating silk veils, such as those worn by Kate Middleton and Kate Moss, suit hair down and hair half up. If you are a fan of big voluminous hairstyles, a stiffer, ruched tulle veil may suit you better. If you fancy an up-do or have shorter hair, a less traditional short birdcage veil can work perfectly. Consider whether you are having a blusher or veil covering your face as you enter the ceremony. If you are wearing a headpiece with the veil, such as a hairband, tiara or flowers, this may be attached to the veil or be separate so you can take the veil off later in the day but still have something on your head.

Do some veils require a particular hairstyle or are most versatile regards fixing?

Different hairstyles suit different veil styles. Most veils have plastic or metal at the top to attach to the hair and additional hairgrips would be used to hold it in place. It is important to consider the position in which the veil will be attached onto your head; you can have it on top towards the face, towards the back of the head or lower down at the back of the head under an up-do hairstyle.

THE HAIR

IT is beguiling to see a bride with hair loose and glossy, perhaps just embellished with a beautiful clip or fascinator, but until fairly recently free-flowing locks have been an unfamiliar wedding sight. The great fun with a vintage wedding is that it can be interpreted in so many ways, leaving room for everything from a rustic, low-key affair to something grand and formal. Your style of dress and hair is likely to reflect this choice, but you don't have to be restricted. An immaculate chignon or pin curls can be perfect in some instances, whilst loose plaits or a softly tousled bun could be the ideal finish to a simple rustic wedding. Personally, I think the splendour and formality of a ravishing wedding dress with soft and unfussy hair works beautifully and this style is very much in vogue at the moment. There are also delectable pieces of vintage and vintage-inspired hair jewellery available and even simple fabric flowers or freshly cut flowers as hair decoration are enough to transform you into the prettiest bride.

➤ *This bride's hair has been softly curled and secured with a 1930s pearl hair comb.*
This loose hairstyle works perfectly with the high collar of this 1970s lace dress.

Hair Adornment

When I married I hunted high and low for pretty fabric flowers for my hair and eventually bought tiny silk lilies of the valley from America. After a thousand possibilities I had my hair down with these flowers clipped in place and this felt enough. How far you go is very much down to personal taste and the choice is endless. There is a list of suppliers in the Where to Find section, pointing you in the direction of everything decorative for your hair, from simple to more creative. The images that follow should give you ideas to trial yourself, including how to create your own beehive hairstyle.

← *A 1940s brooch used as hair decoration.*

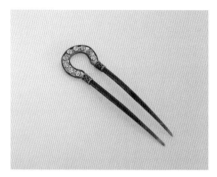

← *Companies such as Vintage Bridal Jewellery have an incredible selection of one-off pieces, including Art Deco combs and Edwardian slides. A beautiful 1920s tortoiseshell and diamanté hair comb is shown here.*

← *Vintage hair decoration can take many forms, including hair slides, combs, hairbands and tiaras. Many original pieces were made from lovely materials, such as silk, organza, diamanté, feathers and wax. This pretty hair decoration is from the wedding of Kate and Rod Beer, Dorking.*

← Leaf and pearl head decoration by Ecclectic Eccentricity, and flowers by Love Blooms, including ranunculus, astrantia, eucalyptus and silver cineraria. This silk wedding dress is by Simeon Morris, worn with a 1960s lace jacket.

The Vintage Hairstyle

There is the exciting option of going for an authentic retro hairdo and when expertly done there is no question that it will look absolutely breathtaking. Be warned, however, as vintage hairstyling can be a delicate issue. Ideally your hair requires teasing by a deft-fingered professional and preferably the best in the business or as close as you can get. For example, pin curls are a tricky undertaking and if at all possible should be set by a hairdresser who can do it with their eyes shut. Backcombing your hair to within an inch of its life only to smooth it down into the sleek hair of a film star takes a great deal more than luck and courage! So if a carefully orchestrated vintage hairstyle is calling then DIY

isn't necessarily the answer. There are, as with every aspect of your vintage wedding, some very clever stylists out there who can whip your hair into a veritable vintage extravaganza.

Amy Taylor from Flamingo Amy is just one such talent and she knows everything there is to know about styling pin curls, victory rolls and beehives, to name but a few. There is an interview with Amy later in the chapter, revealing the tips and pitfalls you will need to be aware of when opting for a vintage hairstyle. If you wish to emulate any of these looks there are specific products that are best suited to certain styles. Your basic kit needs to include hairspray, a boar bristle brush, plenty of hairgrips and curl clips, and a good comb.

← This look is based on a 1930s finger wave but with a modern twist. The style is created with Marcel wave heated tongs and curling clips. Originally Marcel wave tongs would have been heated over the fire, resulting in terrible damage to the hair. Thankfully there are perfectly safe, modern alternatives and protective products that make heat styling much less damaging.

➤ *This classic Hollywood set in the style of Veronica Lake or Lana Turner is an absolute head turner. Soft curls are produced with tongs and curl clips and brushed out to create a glossy, bouncy 1940s finish. Veronica Lake would have had hers completely covering one eye.*

← ↓ The classic beehive is so evocative of the 1960s and when done well looks incredible. This beehive has been swept up at the back and twisted into place, which is great if you have very long hair. However, this style can be adapted to shoulder-length hair and still be secured neatly at the back. In our image we've left the fringe soft to frame the face.

The Modern Alternative

You may feel that choosing an exact replica of a vintage hairstyle may be a step too far. An antique dress might be just enough for any girl and your hair doesn't have to follow suit. How you look on your day is about expressing who you are and if you are keen to have loose, natural hair alongside a 1900s dress then do so, even if it's not in keeping with a bride from that era. It may be a mistake to attempt something too adventurous with your hair for your wedding day, especially if you don't normally experiment, as you may risk looking a bit forced and uncomfortable. It's important to think carefully about your whole look and what will work. If your dress is heavily detailed and intricate then try not to pitch your hair in competition against it. On the other hand if you want a 1950s film star look from head to toe then be brave. Just make sure it all still feels like you underneath, rather than being talked into something that feels unnatural. My advice would be to ensure you have at least one hair trial before your day. This may seem like an obvious decision, but it's surprising how many brides I've spoken to that have expressed their dislike of their wedding hair.

There are plenty of retro-inspired hairstyles that can be done by your hairdresser or even a friend, so do experiment. You could opt for a more natural, unstructured look, including buns, pretty braids and soft waves. These are styles that will complement the vintage look, but without the structure of a slavishly period hairstyle, which may suit you better if you aren't trying to emulate a particular era to the nth degree. For example, Kate Moss' recent wedding gown was very much inspired by dresses of the 1930s, despite being a modern creation by John Galliano. There is no question that a 30s bride would almost certainly have had her hair up, carefully styled and pinned. Kate, however, chose to wear her hair down, which didn't stick to the rules but worked beautifully and she looked serene and comfortable in her skin.

← *From the wedding of Kat and Nick Hirst, Essex. Kat's hair has been softly pinned up and secured with a pretty hair pin.*

↓ *In this hairstyle, a single plait has been secured over the crown and dotted with fresh daisies. This is a lovely soft look if you would like your hair up but still in a relaxed style.*

How to...

CREATE A BEEHIVE HAIRSTYLE

This style is relatively straightforward to attempt yourself but is perhaps easier if you have another pair of hands to help you. Make sure your hair is clean and brushed through. Heat your tongs to the correct temperature for your hair type, which will vary according to the thickness of your hair. You will need: rat tail comb, boar bristle hairbrush, large and small curl clips, hairgrips (Kirby grips), hairspray and heated tongs.

1. Divide the hair into three sections – the first from ear to ear over the crown and two smaller sections at either side of the head. Using large curl clips, secure each section out of the way until needed later (see picture 1).

2. Release the back section of hair and taking small amounts, brush it straight and spray with hairspray. Carefully curl this section and secure it in place using a small curl clip (2). Repeat this process until the whole back section is set into curls (3). You could leave your hair straight at the back, but the soft curls give it a little more body, which balances nicely with the beehive shape.

3. Next take each side section in turn and repeat the curling process as in step 2. Ensure these curls are rolled facing away from the fringe or forehead (4).

4. After about ten minutes, release the back section of curls and brush with a boar bristle brush or loosen with your fingers (5), depending on the look you would like to achieve and how well your hair type will hold a curl.

5. Release the remaining set curls at the front of the head from their clips. Hold each curl vertically (this is where a second pair of hands comes in handy), spray the roots of the hair with a little hairspray and comb from about 5cm (2in) down towards the scalp, ensuring the backcombing is pushed firmly down to the roots (6). Work your way around this section until each curl has been released and backcombed. Start with the top section and then gently do the sides and blend them in. Don't be alarmed if your hair looks pretty unruly at this stage – all will be well I assure you. Once complete, gently brush the hair into place creating the shape that you want using your boar bristle brush. Only brush the outside of your 'structure' to avoid undoing all your backcombing (7).

6. Now you have smoothed and sprayed lightly with hairspray and have the shape you like, pull the hair into a ponytail at the back (8). Twist the ponytail neatly and pin securely with hairgrips (9). Fix the pin firmly by pushing it through from one side, turning it back on itself and securing (10). Comb the fringe into place to finish (11).

Tip

Fresh flowers or a decorative hair clip would be a stunning addition to the back of this beehive and will also cover any visible hair pins.

An interview with...
FLAMINGO AMY

Amy Taylor is a skilled specialist hairstylist who works independently in the UK, styling for vintage events and weddings. She has a pop-up salon and also works from Flint Hair Salon in Norwich.

How long have you been styling vintage hair?

I have been styling hair for four years and I came to it through my love of the fashions of the 1930s to 1960s. I have always been interested in styling my own hair and found that I could use my creative side doing this job.

What are the most popular styles at the moment for vintage wedding hair?

A lot of women like to wear their hair down and either curly or wavy, emulating the style of the 1940s and 50s. Equally popular are elaborate 1940s up-dos. However, the 1930s is becoming increasingly sought after, with soft finger waves.

How important is the hairstyle to your overall look on your wedding day?

Choosing the right style brings all of the elements of your look together; it can give you confidence and make you feel beautiful. Having your hair done makes you feel (and look) like a film star, and what girl doesn't want to feel this way?

How many trial appointments should you book for a vintage wedding hairstyle?

I like to see my bride for a consultation when they book – this could be up to 18 months before the wedding. We can then talk about what sort of hairstyles the bride likes and what she may need to do with her hair leading up to her wedding day to achieve her ideal style. I like to do one trial around eight weeks before the wedding where we try out two styles. Some hairdressers do this much further in advance, but this means the hair will be roughly the same length and condition as it will be on the wedding day, which is important when re-creating a chosen style.

How much would you consider the choice of veil or dress before choosing your style?

Usually a bride has chosen a dress, so the hairstyle would be created around the dress style, her preferences, i.e., wants hair on the face, down and so on, but also by what she wants to wear in her hair. The style has to make allowances for and complement the hair slide, band or veil. For example, if you are wearing a bouffant style you won't usually be able to wear your veil at the front.

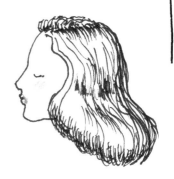

Are certain looks dictated by your hair length or can most styles be adapted?

Longer hair can be more versatile and made to appear shorter for down styles and it is possible to create a 'faux bob'. I would say it is better to have hair longer than you think you'll need it rather than shorter, as if you opt for a curly or wavy style your hair loses about a third of its length. If you are looking for a Marilyn Monroe type of style then your hair needs to be cut in a specific way to achieve this look.

What are the names of classic vintage styles that I could choose from?

People usually name a film star or celebrity from the time, such as Audrey Hepburn, Rita Hayworth or Marilyn Monroe to describe the hairstyle that they would like. The hairstyles do have names though, such as the beehive, victory rolls, pageboy or finger wave.

Which are the easiest styles to try yourself and which require a professional?

Undone beehive styles are relatively easy to do yourself, but more elaborate styles, such as 1930s finger waves and 1940s up-dos, require a professional due to their complexity.

Do you need specific brushes and products for specific vintage hairstyles?

I use modern tools to create a vintage look as it is much quicker to create them this way. I always carry tongs, Tresemmé Freeze Hold hairspray and a boar bristle brush. These brushes are ideal for all hairstyling, whichever era. They can smooth down stray hairs with the help of hairspray and brush out a set to remove the hairspray to give a softer appearance.

THE MAKE-UP

DURING the Victorian era no self-respecting female would deign to be seen with a painted face: at most a lady would perhaps have worn a little light face powder and given her cheeks a quick pinch. Full-scale make-up was reserved for actresses and courtesans, and it wasn't until 1910 onwards that make-up began to lose its poor reputation. Around this time mascara and pancake face make-up made their first appearance, with names such as Max Factor and Maybelline emerging. From then on make-up literally exploded into the public consciousness and make-up boundaries have been pushed ever since. It's useful to look back through the decades and see how making up has changed. Once again, a vintage wedding doesn't mean 'vintage everything' but it can be fun to experiment with different styles, perhaps picking details from various eras to get the look you want. Any good, self-respecting make-up artist skilled in the art of vintage will know exactly what looks were used and how to achieve them and so you can just enjoy experimenting.

➤ *You will definitely want to touch up your make-up throughout the day/ evening so make sure you have a little pot of lipstick or rouge tucked away. From the wedding of Charlie and Darryl Aldous, Brasteds, Norfolk.*

Make-up Artists

An experienced make-up artist may be your safest option if you want to achieve a specific and dramatic look, but there are also companies that sell products for you to use at home, one of which is The Vintage Cosmetic Company. They even have videos that show you how to use all their products, including the application of false eyelashes. The Powderpuff Girls do it all, including a boutique salon where you can have your hair and make-up done professionally, and also an online shop stocking a treasure trove of vintage goodies for hair and make-up for you to try at home. Later in this chapter there is an interview with Katie Reynolds at The Powderpuff Girls, where she offers really useful tips and advice.

Vintage Make-up Styles by Era

Once you have a general idea of the different vintage looks that can be achieved you can start to think about how this ties in with the rest of your styling. Again, there are no rules, so you can experiment with how far you want to take your look. It's worth considering how you feel about wearing make-up generally though. Some of us are used to a fully made-up face on a daily basis, but for others it's a completely alien concept to apply foundation, blusher and mascara.

The 1920s Face
A look made famous by Louise Brooks, Clara Bow and Lillian Gish. Cupid's bow lips were synonymous with the roaring twenties, which accentuated the upper and lower lip but de-accentuated the length of the mouth, giving a doll-like appearance. Lip colours were often strong and dark and eyes were dark lined with fine drawn-in brows. The face itself was pale in colour and popular blush colours were rose pink and orange.

The 1930s Face
A look made famous by Greta Garbo, Marlene Dietrich and Mae West. Pale pinky-toned foundation with little or no blush. Eyebrows were plucked very finely or even shaved and then drawn in with a high arch. Eyeshadow colours were vibrant purples and greens and for evening were used right up to the brow line to startling effect. False eyelashes were also popular. Lips were painted full with a Cupid's bow curve at the edges and bright red was favoured.

The 1940s Face
A look made famous by Ava Gardner, Rita Heyworth and Betty Grable. The trend that emerged during the 1940s was for a warmer glow with rosy pink cheeks, in contrast to the paler faces of the 1920s and 30s. Eyebrows were left slightly more natural but were still drawn in to create definition in a long arch. Lips were full and in varying shades of bright and orangey red, but eyes were much more muted, using eyeshadows in browns and greys.

← *Don't think you have to apply a look that makes you feel ill at ease or too heavily made-up. Vintage looks can be toned down so that you are still true to an era but not completely overtaken by it. From the wedding of Tricia and Toby Nevitt, Powder Rooms, Columbia Road, London.*

The 1950s Face

A look made famous by Elizabeth Taylor, Audrey Hepburn and Marilyn Monroe. The term 'bombshell' was coined and Hollywood stars were in full make-up bloom. The face was pale and interesting. Black, cat-like liquid liner accentuated the lash line and arched, defined brows were standard. The top lip was over accentuated for a sultry pout and red lips were the order of the day. The beauty spot made a comeback, placed near the mouth or eye.

The 1960s Face

A look made famous by Catherine Deneuve, Jane Fonda and Twiggy. In the 1960s there was a literally a style revolution and this was no more evident than the faces of women throughout the decade. It was all about the eyes and perhaps more pointedly, the eyelashes. Pale faces and pale lips were very much in vogue, in contrast with dark striking eyes and frosted eyeshadows. Again, cat-like liquid eyeliner was a huge trend.

The 1970s Face

A look made famous by Farrah Fawcett and Goldie Hawn. The time of discos and hippies! The more dramatic of the 70s make-up look was dominated by false eyelashes and the ubiquitous frosted blue eyeshadow. Lips were pale and often just with a high gloss and faces were minimally covered, more usually with tinted moisturizer rather than a heavy foundation for a very natural look. Blush tended to be shimmery and soft.

An interview with...

THE POWDERPUFF GIRLS

The Powderpuff Girls was founded in 2005 by make-up artist Katie Reynolds. With over ten years extensive experience in the film, television and fashion arena, Katie saw a niche for a team of talented make-up artists, hairstylists, manicurists and massage therapists, all beautifully turned out in 1950s-inspired uniforms in true old-fashioned, silver screen style.

How far in advance do I need to book a consultation and should I bring a picture of the make-up look I like?

At least two weeks in advance is essential. It's helpful to bring a file of looks you like, so your make-up artist can get a good idea about your style. Make sure you take into account any holidays, facials or sun beds you may have booked before the actual day and let your make-up artist know, as this may make a difference to the skincare routine and foundation she chooses.

How much time is booked for a make-up trial?

Usually a couple of hours, but it could be less if you have a definite idea of what you want, or longer if you are undecided. This trial is an opportunity to perfect your look, to try out your different ideas and there is no strict time limit for this (within reason!). We can travel to you, or you can come to us at one of our venues.

What is the most popular vintage look for brides?

At the moment the most popular looks are 1920s and 1940s, but things change all the time. Most people seem to choose the 1920s for the dress style with just a nod towards the 20s with hair and make-up, as the make-up was usually a gorgeous dark smoky eye and a very deep, dark berry lip in a little rosebud shape, which is quite a dramatic look for a wedding but fabulous if you are brave enough to go for it. 1940s make-up is much easier to wear as it is quite light on the eye and is all about the strong red lips. An easy bridal look is the 1950s, as pastels were very popular and suit those brides who want to go for something more traditionally bridal, natural and rosy looking. Lips were a softer more coral red or pink; much sheerer and less matte than the 1940s.

What are the most important factors when deciding on vintage-style wedding make-up?

It is very helpful if you have already chosen your dress, as some looks may work better with a certain era of dress. But you don't need to stick to the make-up of the decade. For example, a 1940s dress would be set off very well with a good, strong matte red lipstick, but this might not suit you or you may feel this is too strong a look for your wedding. Having your dress already can really help you get a picture of the finished look, as a lovely vintage make-up could feel odd if you are in jeans and T-shirt. It's your wedding so it's up to you – we are just here to help you find a look that suits you.

Can you do the make-up for the rest of my wedding party?

Yes we can indeed! We are happy to do bridesmaids, flower girls, mothers of the bride and best friends. We wouldn't normally do a trial for the rest of the wedding party.

Do you sell the make-up that you use in case I want to re-touch throughout the day?

Yes we do have a small selection in our online shop, and your make-up artist can also make a list for you of items she thinks you might need on the day. A pressed powder and a lipstick are two essential items for your bridal purse.

Can you teach me how to do my own wedding hair or make-up?

Yes, you could come in for a lesson prior to your wedding. Make sure you give yourself plenty of time to practise and perfect your newly learned skills before the big day!

How can I avoid getting make-up on my dress?

It is always best to step into your dress if possible after your hair and make-up is done. If it absolutely has to go over your head then you can put a chiffon or silk scarf over your whole head covering your face and get someone to help you on with your dress as this is tricky!

THE JEWELLERY

NOWHERE in this book seems more of an appropriate home for the wedding phrase, 'something old, something new, something borrowed, something blue'. Some wonderful wedding traditions never fade and this one has remained constant throughout the years. Jewellery is the ideal way to weave a family heirloom into your day and this is when true vintage finery really comes into its own. A bracelet, necklace or earrings handed down through generations, or even a single piece that was perhaps worn by a mother or grandmother, can imbue an item with genuine meaning. How much jewellery you choose is very much down to personal taste but often one or two pieces can be enough, particularly if your dress or veil is intricate and detailed or you have some hair decoration. You may have the good fortune to have a family member or friend who can proffer a piece of jewellery that works with your chosen look. Of course this good luck doesn't befall every bride, but that just means another chance to have fun looking, and perhaps unearth a beautiful heirloom that can be passed on to your own children.

➤ *A collection of beautiful painted china brooches from the 1950s.*

Old, New, Borrowed, Blue

A wedding photographer recently told me how common it was for brides to change their minds about jewellery choices on their wedding morning. A bride tends to have made firm decisions about her hair, make-up, dress and veil well in advance of her nuptials. Jewellery on the other hand is something small enough to be dispensed with or changed at the last moment. It is highly probable that your wedding morning is the first time you have tried every aspect of your look together including hair, make-up and accessories, so your feelings can definitely change when your look is complete. Bearing this in mind it might be worthwhile sourcing one or two pieces that you like, which gives you the chance to be as fickle as you choose on your wedding morning.

True Vintage

When choosing wedding jewellery you want to make a statement that doesn't jostle for the limelight with your wedding dress but sets it off to perfection This is an exciting opportunity if you are a vintage lover because vintage jewellery can be just divine, easy to come by and often not costing a fortune. Vintage weddings don't necessarily mean thrifty weddings, so it's great to find pieces that aren't madly expensive. Flea markets and antique fairs are ten a penny these days and wonderful places to pick up accessories. You can also use vintage pieces in many different ways to great effect. For example, brooches can be attached to hair combs and worn in your hair. There are even brooch bouquets available from DC Bouquets – see The Flowers section.

← *1930s gold watch bracelet.*

↓ *1920s wire-covered fabric necklace with early painted plastic flowers.*

➤ *Edwardian-style costume jewellery in black jet.*

↓ *Pretty costume jewellery adds interest to a simple bodice.*

Vintage with a Modern Twist

Of course your jewellery doesn't necessarily need to be an original vintage creation and there are some exquisite alternative options. There are companies who design and create marvellous vintage-style jewellery with a modern edge: one such independent business is Eclectic Eccentricity. Their range is impeccable and the stock spans from classical pieces to items with a whimsical, light-hearted edge. The selection is also sizeable and well-priced. Some of their clever signature pieces can be seen in our bridesmaid images. They also have a carefully hand-selected range of original vintage pieces.

The high street is also awash with absolutely fantastic costume jewellery these days. Your wedding jewellery doesn't have to cost a fortune and once teamed with your heavenly dress, it can be hard to tell the difference.

Reinvented and Remade

There are alternatives to original items and a handful of clever companies use vintage pieces and reinvent them, or will even design pieces for you utilizing old stones or settings. This is a great way to have something very personal and meaningful made. This type of up-cycling is very popular and a lovely way to breathe new life into an antique that may just be gathering dust. The Vintage Jewellery Company is one such set-up and they have a striking selection of unique pieces to choose from. Laurel Lime also works to transform old pieces into new and inspiring accessories for the vintage-conscious bride.

↑ *1920s full-length diamanté earrings.*

↓ *Green Bakelite clip-on bracelet from the 1930/40s.*

Jewellery Styles by Era

1920s and 1930s Jewellery

There are so many quintessential 1920s fashion looks and many of these translate wonderfully to your vintage wedding day. Long layered strings of pearls or beads and geometric Art Deco designs dominated the period. Bracelets were often worn en masse due to the fall in popularity of evening gloves. Earrings were predominantly shoulder length as hair was kept fashionably short in the bob style. Pearls, diamanté and marcasite were all having their day. This style of jewellery continued to be popular well into the 1930s too, but necklace lengths were shortened and earrings tended to be rather more stud-like than the long, dangling pieces of the 1920s.

1940s and 1950s Jewellery

Bakelite became a very popular material for jewellery making in the 1940s. It was both versatile and inexpensive, which meant it could be produced in a wonderful array of designs and colours for everyday wear. However, in the post-war years, glamour and opulence was creeping back into the public consciousness and large gemstones and rose gold were often used in statement pieces, such as brooches and necklaces, if they could be afforded. Diamanté could be set into Bakelite jewellery, instantly making it a beguiling yet a less expensive alternative to diamonds, and rhinestones were often used in place of real gems. It could be pretty hard to tell the difference between the real thing and its less expensive counterpart. Pearls also made their reappearance in the 50s, worn short but often multi-stranded.

1960s and 1970s Jewellery

The jewellery of this period threw caution to the wind in comparison to the more formal decoration of earlier times. Bib necklaces became popular, shoulder-length chandelier earrings and long necklaces were back with a vengeance. Plastic was popular too, with bold flower designs and geometric patterns. Asymmetrical design, strong colour and a deliberately eclectic style was favoured, so often a multitude of designs and textures were worn.

➜ *1960s gold leather bracelet.*

➜ ↓ *1960s two-string pearls with diamanté clasp.*

↓ *Costume jewellery pearl bracelet.*

THE GROOM

IN reality a 'vintage groom' is a bit of a confusing label simply because grooms of yesteryear would have worn a very traditional matching, smart and low-key ensemble. It appears though that at last grooms are finally shaking off the stiff formalities and constraints of the formulaic male wedding attire that we have come to know and yawn at. Now is the renaissance of the groom. In between those years of the traditional and rather beautiful timeless suits of the 1930s and 40s we have managed to stumble upon a modern groom who tends to underwhelm us in a somewhat dubious waistcoat, outrageously shiny shoes and rather a good deal of pale pink, not to mention the squeaky clean shave. No longer! It's time for our gentlemen to step to the fore and make their own sense of style known.

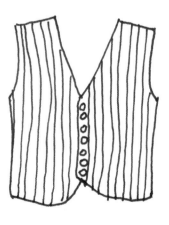

➤ This groom wears an Old Town silk tie, Gibson waistcoat and shirt from Elements.
This is a perfect example of the vintage gentleman – with not a matching fabric in sight.

→ *Gibson jacket, shirt by Farah Vintage and bow tie by Scotch and Soda, all from Elements clothing shop.*

→ ↓ *A pair of well-worn and polished brown boots looks stylish and relaxed.*

The Vintage Groom

For today's vintage groom, it doesn't matter if your suit is green or your shoes are brown, if your hair is a little unkempt or you want to wear a straw hat. Braces, britches, cord, work-wear, bow ties and beards are all okay too, and at the risk of sounding trite, why should the girls get all the fun? It's not that I'm suggesting grubby trousers or an ill-fitting jacket, just that the groom should be allowed to express himself as much as his bonny bride, and rather than becoming the prop he becomes exactly what he should be – the partner!

Of course, a dashing, sharp suit that fits like a dream is a thing to behold, but for heaven's sake make it interesting. Navy blue slim-fitting suits with brown lace-up shoes are standing out as the suit du jour on the wedding merry-go-round, but if you prefer something a little more informal then ditch the jacket altogether and wear a pair of braces. Bow ties can look brilliant, as can a stylish, patterned cotton tie in a lovely fabric, such as gingham or liberty lawn. Even plimsolls, retro sunglasses, fob watches and hats, from trilbies to berets, are making their presence felt. So let the festivities begin!

already mentioned, a three-piece suit is by no means the only option. A pair of wonderful vintage trousers can be teamed with a new shirt, or braces, a mismatched jacket or a waistcoat. Either way, the whole search can be great fun and you get as many shopping trips as your wife-to-be, which seems only just.

Seek and Ye Shall Find

Finding an original vintage wedding suit that fits and looks pristine may be a little like finding hens' teeth but if you manage to hunt one down it will be worth it; mainly because compared to a new suit it will cost less money, but it will very likely be made in notably finer fabric, lined beautifully and probably will be in good condition. This is simply because suits that have survived through the years would have been those kept for Sunday best on the whole. On balance, unlike the vintage wedding dress, which has taken the world by storm, there still aren't very many places to find vintage clothing for men, which means there are limited treasure troves to rummage through. On the other hand, as I've

Vintage-inspired Grooms

The first place I'm going to mention is not actually an outfit selling vintage clothing, but rather it sells new clothing that takes its inspiration from useful, functional garments from history. Old Town will make you giddy with excitement if this look is your thing. The website explains beautifully their ethos, so I've quoted it here. 'To the casual observer Old Town might appear to be simply an exercise in nostalgia, but we hope that the discerning might notice that the garments are essentially useful items with reference points and influences from past costume. In much the same way as today's townscape is made of elements from different periods, we attempt in a simple way, to play with the notion of Now and Then.'

↑ *Gibson suit, Old Town silk tie and button down fine check shirt by Knowledge Cotton Apparel from Elements clothing shop.*

↑ *Your hair, shoes and accessories will inform your whole look. Despite wearing a modern shirt and waistcoat, there is a slightly bohemian, dandy vintage look to this groom, thanks to his relaxed navy blue vintage suit and Old Town tie. The bride wears a vintage Edwardian cream wedding dress with parasol.*

This shop is a veritable clothing bazaar, including silk ties designed in-house, trousers, jackets, waistcoats and shirts in an array of designs and tempting fabrics, such as cavalry drill, Irish linen, wool serge and corduroy, to name but a few. Braces, shoes and belts are carefully selected to complement these functional yet impossibly stylish pieces. This is the perfect choice if you're looking for something slightly less formal but that makes a very particular statement, and ideal to mix in with other pieces both old and new.

Authentic Looks

Of course, there are some amazing vintage men's shops that are essential to list here. Tweedmans Vintage is a perfect example. This Lincolnshire-based company ship worldwide and have a fabulous range of vintage suits and accessories to choose from. Their stock is constantly changing and the website is divided into sections and eras for ease of use.

Another absolute must to look at is Savvy Row. This company specializes in high quality vintage suits and accessories from the pre-1930s to the 1970s. Names such as Burberry, Harris Tweed and Savile Row are available, amongst others, and there is a huge selection. Great attention to detail is paid to each listing, which makes an online purchase much less dicey. They also have a good returns policy.

Modern and Magnificent

The alternative to this vintage hunting is to wear a modern suit. Just as with wedding dresses there is a huge range of suits available that you could be forgiven for thinking were from a bygone era. There is no reason why a groom sporting a modern tweed suit, such as the one shown in the photograph above, can't look like he's a cutting-edge vintage groom.

THE BRIDESMAIDS

WHEN it comes to bridesmaid dresses, particularly for adults, there are a number of fantastic possibilities that fall under the vintage banner. Of course there is 'the original vintage dress', which is the absolute Holy Grail, but this is going to prove awfully tricky if you want your bridesmaids to wear identical frocks – in fact, nigh on impossible. There is a chance that you may only have one bridesmaid, which makes life much simpler. However, it's probably more likely that you will have at least two bridesmaids, or more, which adds a whole new dimension to your search. You could potentially choose a period in history, for example the 1950s, and look for a selection of dresses that fall into this era. This would give your girls a chance to express their own personalities and also to feel comfortable in a dress that suits their body type.

➤ *Two stunning vintage wedding dresses 1970s (left) and 1930s (right). The flower girl wears a new dress by I Love Gorgeous. A white paper flower crown was made by Suzi Mclaughlin.*

To Match or Not to Match

Just as the bride has body hang-ups, the bridesmaids will
too, and if you choose a slim-fitting bias-cut 1920s dress and
one of your bridesmaids has 'bottom issues', there may be
the odd crisis of confidence. There is nothing worse than
a bridesmaid who loathes her dress! By broadly selecting
your favoured fashion period there is scope to make sure
everyone feels fabulous. Choose carefully so that the dresses
complement one another or have a common theme, so there
is some continuity. The obvious choice here is to select a
colour. This can mean a stunning selection of original dresses
that suit their wearer but also ensure that everyone looks like
they're going to the same wedding.

If you are opting for solely old, bear in mind that sizing
was very different 50 years ago. Dresses were often smaller so
if your girls vary in size this may require some super sleuth
hunting, so give yourself plenty of time! If this seems like too
much of a tall order then you can employ the skilled eye of
Abigail at Abigail's Vintage Bridal. She will source vintage
dresses for you that differ in style but are tonally the same and
there are some great examples shown on her website.

*← We have put these bridesmaids into off-white dresses. One
dress is contemporary with a vintage edge and the other is vintage
silk with hand smocking, but they work wonderfully together.*

← *These bridesmaids are wearing modern high street dresses, coupled with handmade navy blue felt berets by Annelli Clarke, and belted with vintage plaited leather belts. The girls are wearing 1940s original shoes and cream lace tights.*

Off the Peg

If the original dress hunt feels too much like an uphill struggle we come to the slightly less stressful option of buying off the peg. These days vintage fashion has so permeated our everyday lives that we are spoilt for choice on the high street. Everything from 1920s flapper dresses, 1940s tea dresses, 1960s mini dresses to 1970s maxi dresses are in abundance. This can be wonderful, three-fold: one, because you can find some splendid stuff; two, because you're not going to have to spend a small fortune to make your bridesmaids look fantastic and three, you can choose the same dress for everyone. Incidentally, another fantastic option is to take a look at the fabulous 1950s-inspired dresses from What Katie Did. Pin-up girl Bernie Dexter has designed a range of stunning frocks that would serve beautifully as bridesmaid dresses. The fabrics are fantastic, the 1950s shape is forgiving on most body shapes and they come in a wide range of sizes.

New Dress, Vintage Touches

You could choose a simple high street or wedding shop dress for all your girls but then embellish with wonderful vintage accessories, such as fabric flowers, sequins, buttons, bows, jewellery, belts, clutches and so on.

→ *These two pink spotty mesh dresses with button detailing are by Dahlia, in the sale at £18 each. Although modern they have a vintage feel and look perfect twinned with antique accessories. Vintage glass necklaces, matching paper flowerhead combs and bottle green suede peep-toe shoes by Ravel complete the look.*

Made To Order

The third string to your bow is making or having your dresses made, which gives you carte blanche to really indulge your vintage passion. It also means you can choose matching dresses whatever age or size your bridesmaids are, which can even be tricky when high street shopping. Have a look at the Sew Direct website and click on the Vogue Vintage Pattern section to find an exciting array of stunning vintage dress patterns that will set your pulse racing – and these patterns are brand new. Incidentally, you can still find heavenly original patterns for dresses at antique fairs and in second-hand shops, so keep your eyes peeled on those antique shop hunting trips.

If you're a dab hand with a sewing machine then this could provide you with the perfect bridesmaids dress choice. However, if you're not confident at sewing or simply don't want the extra work and you are going for something truly authentic and complicated it is imperative that you find a seamstress who is skilled in the art of dealing with or making replica dresses. There may be boning or bias cutting involved and this requires skill to ensure the finished result looks perfect. One such seamstress is Anne Barclay. Anne makes replica dresses with a modern twist and they are absolutely exquisite. Having a dress made also means expert judgements about the style choice of your dresses, particularly if there are lots of different body types to be dressed.

Of course this doesn't mean you have to hire someone experienced in haute couture to achieve a fabulous look. There may be somebody in your circle of friends or family who can sew or there is likely to be a local seamstress in your area. Bridesmaid dresses don't need to be madly complicated either and can be very low cost when homemade. Just choosing a simple shift dress pattern in pretty broderie anglaise or cotton gingham can work if cleverly accessorized, and having homemade aspects to your wedding adds such charm and individuality.

→ *Our pretty flower girl wears a 1960s vintage dress and a wire headdress, courtesy of Annelli Clarke. Flowers by Love Blooms include craspedia, lisianthus, silver cineraria and eucalyptus.*

← *This original 1940s crêpe dress with tie belt looks fantastic and requires little more than a pair of heavenly shoes and some pretty flowers.*

Flower Girls

The same rules apply to the smaller version of your bridal entourage – it's either original, off the peg or made for you. In recent years the revival of the vintage wedding dress has meant a multitude of companies popping up, giving you a huge range and breadth of possibilities for your wedding gown. Not so for the humble flower girl, I'm afraid. It may be hard to find children's vintage clothing in good condition that would befit your smaller bridesmaids so you're going to have to look hard. However, you can have such fun with children's clothes for weddings, because they love dressing up. There are so many beautiful high street choices, but also wonderful vintage possibilities, and these were often handmade, which makes them all the more beguiling.

There are some magnificent boutiques, such as I Love Gorgeous, Bonpoint and Eden's Bouquet, which will make choosing virtually impossible if you're looking for something new but so different from the run-of-the-mill bridesmaid dresses. If you do decide to have something made, then old fabric can make a wonderful new dress. If you know somebody who can sew then scour your local antique fairs and even jumble sales for pretty bits of vintage fabric – even curtains and bedspreads, when deconstructed, can be transformed into a pretty child's frock. One incredible company called Best of Youth make exquisite bridesmaid dresses using pure silk, cotton, linen and wool. Dresses are hand finished with vintage lace and hand embroidered linen and any dyeing required uses plant dyes. Each dress is unique and can be tailor made.

↑ *Delightful floral dresses in a simple design work perfectly here. It adds to their charm that the fabrics have an identical print but are different colours.*

There are so many delightful touches for the child bridesmaid, including twisted willow headbands, daisy chains, ribbons and bows for the hair, handmade bags for petals and tiny flower hoops or bouquets with simple country flowers. This is a chance to indulge your every whim and at least for the initial stages of your wedding have your bridesmaids looking perfect. Things may deteriorate in the style stakes later on, with the addition of hide and seek coupled with chocolate ice cream, but by that time it won't matter a jot.

THE STATIONERY

YOUR beautiful invitations are going to drop ceremoniously onto the mat of every one of your shared friends and family members and you want it to speak volumes about your forthcoming wedding day. And if you are very well organized then perhaps a 'save the date' card will precede it. The possibilities for invitations are infinite and can seem a little overwhelming. Everything from very traditional to quirky and stylized, printed or homemade is feasible but it can be a hard decision to make especially when two of you are making it. At this stage you may also be in the relatively early throws of your wedding planning so you may not have found your style stride yet. However, if you know that you would like something vintage-inspired then you will find some fabulous ideas in the following pages to point you in the right direction. I think the key to vintage is often its simplicity and as soon as you start thinking about what could be incorporated you can simply enjoy yourself.

➤ *Memorable, personalized stationery designed by I Like Pens.*

MENU

Starter
PEA AND HAM SOUP WITH SOURDOUGH BREAD

Main
PICKERINGS SAUSAGES WITH MASH AND ONION GRAVY

Dessert
APPLE TART WITH HOMEMADE ICECREAM

SAVE THE DATE

R ♥ 6.10.2012

POSTCARD

R.S.V.P

↑ *For my wedding invitations we used pretty vintage stamps to create a design, drew a simple map and found a local printing company to do the rest.*

↑ *Letterpress printing has a captivating, tactile finish that looks both thoroughly handcrafted, yet impossibly stylish. This example is by Strawberry Sorbet.*

Homemade Invitations

Pretty fabric, old lace, buttons, ribbon, pressed flowers and exemplary drawing or handwriting are all ideal if you want to do something a little homespun, although perhaps not all on the same card! If you're somebody who loves making things this can be a chance to indulge your creativity.

Inking stamps are a relatively stress-free way of creating something yourself without needing a degree in graphic design. If this still seems a daunting task there are lots of clever designers and artists who make exquisite stationery, and these days the choice is as diverse as it is fabulous.

Letterpress Printing

Letterpress is a printing technique dating back to the 15th century. The process involves inking the surface of movable type or blocks and pressing them onto a surface. Letterpress prints are crisp and inherently tactile compared to other printing techniques because of the impression into the paper, giving greater visual definition. A letterpress print has a wonderfully delicate impression that you can't help but run your fingers over. When you hold a letterpress invite you get a real sense of quality, nostalgia and the craftsmanship taken to create each and every print. Letterpress stationery looks, feels and smells like no other!

Letterpress printed stationery is a very popular choice for many vintage-inspired weddings and it's easy to see why. This was the staple form of printing for centuries and although no longer used as standard practice, it is perfect for invitations. There are some expert companies that do this, such as the beautiful Emma Jo, whose website is bursting full of inspiration. You can either choose from a selection of pre-designed ideas or they offer a completely bespoke service. Emma Prescott from Emma Jo has kindly given us an insight into the ordering and design process with her interview later in this section. There is also Bella Figura, a New York-based company who have a lovely ethos and a real commitment to keeping this art form alive. Another expert company that is an absolute must is Strawberry Sorbet. They offer a range of beautifully designed invitations, which can then be adapted to your requirements.

Hand-drawn and Personal

If you're searching for something very personal then look no further than the following companies. The Story House will tell your story visually with charming pencil and watercolour maps of your relationship. These are irresistible and full of personality. Equally as beguiling are the offerings of Wolf Whistle, who will skilfully create personalized portraits of you and your partner, your venue or anything else you can think of.

Another real find is Charlie Scribble. This lovely company will produce heavenly fine line drawings for you that are delicate, individual and full of charm. They offer a completely bespoke service of hand illustrations printed on 100 per cent recycled, eco-friendly paper.

Off the Peg

Of course you could buy your wedding invitations ready to go. You may feel that this eliminates the personal touch somewhat but there are some fabulous stationery designers around who produce beautiful ready-made invitations, and this can be so advantageous if you don't have a huge amount of time, money, or are lacking a bit of visual inspiration.

As an example, look no further than the very talented Lucy Jane Batchelor. The 'Love' section on her website boasts two very beautiful examples of wedding invitations and you simply have to pop them in the post. The company, Wedding in a Teacup, have a splendid array of pre-designed invitations and save the date cards, which you order and are then personalized for you. Speaking of pre-designed, I challenge you not to fall in love with one of the myriad of options on Printable Press, particularly from their hand-drawn range. And as if that wasn't enough, Love vs Design make me want to skip with excitement. Not only do they offer a huge selection of charming, ready to buy wedding invitations but they also provide you with a whole section of free printable designs, from place cards to favour tags.

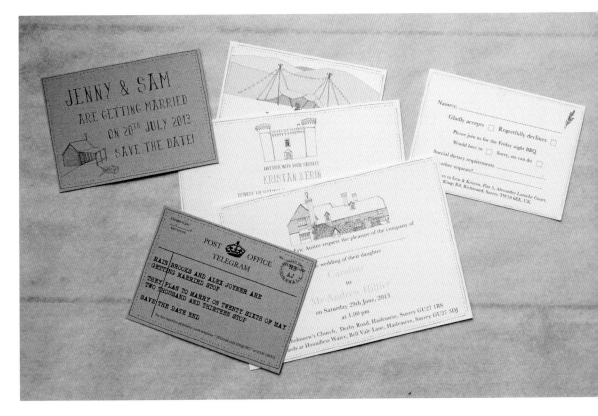

→ *Charlie
Scribble is
responsible for
these delightful
stationery designs
with beautiful pen
and ink drawings.*

An interview with...
EMMA JO

Emma Prescott is a wedding stationery designer and printer, creating innovative and unique wedding stationery in her letterpress studio. She designs and prints everything, offering options, design suggestions and expert advice along the way, so ordering your stationery with Emma Jo is a very personal experience.

. . . .

How far in advance of my wedding should I think about invitations and stationery

Try to begin the process as soon as you can. If you have confirmed your date and venue start thinking about your stationery. Consider designs, order samples, discuss colours and print finishes and if you would like a bespoke design be mindful that a stationer will require additional time for this service. Rushing the process can mean compromising on what you really want. I've had couples who wanted letterpress invitations with beautifully hand-scribed envelopes but left it too late, which is so disappointing. Your stationer is likely to be working on several weddings at once and if you delay ordering they will not be able to turn your invites around instantly. RSVPs confirm how many guests will be attending, something your caterer or venue may need to know, so consider this when sending out your invites. Also, if you would like place cards and table plans you need to allow enough time for them to be designed and checked carefully before being printed.

Can you explain how the bespoke service works?

I love collaborating with couples to create completely original, bespoke stationery that truly reflects them and their special day. Initially, I recommend that the couple spend a little time discussing their ideas, what they want, what they really don't want, while gathering some inspiration. I also love hearing all about them and their journey together as these details really help to capture that personal touch within their stationery. The more they can tell me what they love and hope for, the more I can understand their tastes, suggest ideas and develop them into a solid concept they will love. I devote a lot a time and care to each bespoke project and we can spend a few weeks creating mood boards, finalizing details, materials and finishes. Each project is completely different. After the initial consultation, where we discuss and review ideas and inspiration, I produce an initial proof based on the chosen concept. This is then reviewed, feedback is given and adjustments made, culminating in final approval. We then go to print and assembly if needed.

Roughly how much does an order cost for a set of wedding invitations?

It really depends on your requirements. I offer digital alongside letterpress printed stationery to give my couples flexibility with their budget. You can choose a budget friendly, ready-made design that is customized with your own details, or you can splurge on a fully bespoke design with all the lovely finishing touches. I offer lots of mix and match options that don't compromise on design quality, so if you love letterpress but have a limited budget, have them printed in one ink instead of two. Stationery isn't a priority for every couple but sending beautiful invites to your family and friends hints at the wonderful day ahead.

Can you also design the stationery for the ceremony and reception, for example place setting cards, order of service, table plans and so on?

If it's paper based I love to design it! As well as save the dates and invitations I design and print all 'on the day' stationery, including place cards, menus, order of services and table plans. I have also been asked to design lots of lovely one-off pieces, including thank you signs, favour labels, song request cards, cocktail vouchers, flags, posters and guest books. I love hearing my couple's ideas and tackling different challenges and my designs have even translated through to other elements of the day, including the wedding cake, favour biscuits and even a commemorative coin favour! Stationery can really help bring your wedding theme together and even influence other key decisions in the planning stage.

You offer a calligraphy service too. Does this mean you will individually name and address each invitation?

Yes, invitations, envelopes and place cards individually hand scribed are such a beautiful finishing touch. Receiving a beautifully hand scribed envelope creates the ultimate wow factor!

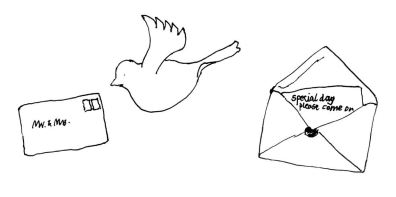

THE LOCATION

SO, you've exclaimed that, 'yes' you would very much like to get married. Your mind is now swimming with a million ideas and counter ideas, and one of those that flash like a beacon for most of us is where on earth is this utopian-splendour of a location? And how am I to find it before the looming date? There are, of course, very lucky people who have friends or relations with magnificent houses, gardens, fields or barns and that question is taken care of in the blink of an eye. However, for most of us this simply isn't the case and a venue will need to be found that exceeds your expectations in so many ways. Is it in the right place, with the right ambience and the right décor, with the right garden and is it the right price? It's a tricky choice indeed – but not impossible.

➤ *An idyllic setting, from the wedding of Kelly and James Alcock, Braziers Park, Reading.*

Finding Your Dream Venue

I have broken this section down into four types of wedding location. This may seem a little limiting because your wedding can and should be a mixture of whatever you fancy, and my ideas of how these should look may well be different to yours. However, this is not a definitive guide but a suggestion of how you might find and create a wedding that loosely reflects each of these. See the Where to Find section at the back of the book for a useful list of fabulous venues.

↓ A tranquil setting that makes imaginative use of a beautiful garden. From the wedding of Kelly and James Alcock, Braziers Park, Reading.

The Homespun Wedding

Ideally the homespun wedding is orchestrated on home turf and preferably in the countryside. It doesn't require an enormous amount of land or a huge house, but you do need to be realistic. It will probably require space for tents or awnings of some kind and will need to be able to accommodate a reasonable amount of guests, unless your event is small and perfectly formed. To be honest, this is probably the wedding that I most hankered after myself, but then was rudely awoken to the reality of our postage stamp of a garden and my parents' city pad, neither of which were quite going to cut the mustard. Having said that, if you haven't got it then you can certainly hire it with a bit of searching.

A new discovery I would like to mention looks just idyllic. The Keeper and the Dell is a wedding location incorporating a beautiful outdoor space called The Dell, but also providing a marquee, a barn and even a camp kitchen. And as if that

↑ *This pretty, intimate little barn is an absolutely perfect choice for a country-style wedding reception. The slightly tumbledown setting all adds to its charm and there are so many wonderful details that can transform such a humble location.*

The Country Barn/ Village Hall Wedding

wasn't enough there is also a wooden cabin with a wood-burning stove, a pretty bell tent and a paddock for camping.

Cow Parsley Farm is family run and provides the idyllic setting of a working farm with all the rustic touches your heart desires. Another lovely spot is Swallow Tail Hill Farm with 16 hectares (40 acres) of wildflower fields and woodland. For me this type of wedding means trestle tables in the meadow, bunting, lanterns and fairy lights in the trees, picnic rugs and deckchairs. Ideally, it is an outdoor event as much as possible, but there are original canvas marquees with wooden poles available to hire, which can house your guests if the good old English weather decides not to be behave. One such resource is Vintage Marquees, who hire out intimate traditional canvas marquees. Alternatively, you could opt for Funky Monkey Tents, which includes the possibility of bell tents, tipis and Bedouin tents. There are a number of other companies listed at the back of the book that can supply all sorts of possibilities for celebrating undercover.

Rustic, frugal and above all covered, seems a preferable alternative when the weather leaves us all a little befuddled. We shot one of our weddings in a beautiful little barn in the Norfolk countryside and all of us involved couldn't help wishing it was our wedding reception taking place that day. I don't quite know why a simple barn becomes so utterly charming when strung with fairy lights, homemade bunting and coloured paper lanterns, but it just does. I think perhaps it has something to do with the transformation of something so visually wonderful out of something so basic. You can also bring the outside in and the inside out with little effort. We put lots of big flower blooms into climbing ivy outside the barn and strung paper pom-poms in the entrance. Fairy lights were both inside and outside the structure, making it magical wherever you spent the day and evening. Jam jars as vases, galvanized buckets for holding drinks, wooden crates and hay bales as seats and huge piles of picnic rugs to keep off the winter chill all add charm to this type of wedding.

Village halls can have a similar effect, as long as they haven't been too modernized. I always feel a bit sad when a village hall upgrades to lino flooring, replacing lovely old floorboards, or a whole new set of plastic chairs to replace the wooden folding ones. I know this is unfair as these are community spaces and need to be accessible and comfortable for all – it's just that they do tend to lose a bit of personality and charm during these transformations. They are still around in their vintage states though and if you find a good one it will probably be extremely reasonable to hire. Definitely have a look at Chichester Hall and also Barrington Park to inspire you. Both of these village halls are astoundingly beautiful and there may just be one tucked away in a village near you.

↓ Voewood House has to be seen to be believed. Each room feels like a different space entirely and, despite the grand exterior of this Arts and Crafts treasure, it also offers a sense of intimacy, which is a marvellous combination.

The Grand House Wedding

Hiring a majestic country pile for the day or weekend is historically a popular wedding choice. However, this can present more problems than it solves. Many of our stunning manor houses and stately homes have been woefully adapted to cater for the wedding market, and dare I say that a good proportion of them have been rather ruined in the process. These elegant, architectural masterpieces become more like a marital production line, and almost insultingly take on more than one wedding at a time to bring in as much revenue as possible. Searching for somewhere that represents your taste and individuality and is a captivating space for your festivities may be an undertaking, but worth it when you find it.

↑ *A most memorable alternative wedding venue, used for the wedding of Kelly and Toby Lane, Wapping Project, London.*

The Retro Chic Alternative Wedding

Amazing and unusual spaces, such as warehouses, railway stations, traditional, stylish old city pubs and even windmills, are making their presence felt on the alternative wedding circuit. We are certainly returning to the notion of intimacy rather than grandeur to celebrate our marital unions, and the boundaries of traditional wedding venues has clearly shifted over the past few years. Don't be afraid of crumbling paint, steel girders or even empty spaces. These are just waiting to be filled with your brilliant ideas and personality. Look no further than MC Motors for a warehouse to die for. If you're after something a little more intimate but still stylish and unusual, you can hire Cley Windmill for your wedding, or The Tin Tabernacle in Oxfordshire, which is literally a beautiful chapel made of tin. Of course, you may prefer your reception on Platform One at Horsebridge Station – it's all there for the taking! See the Where to Find section for website addresses and details of venues.

At the top of my list is Voewood House. Tucked away in the North Norfolk countryside, this original butterfly house idyll is quite simply breathtaking and marvellously idiosyncratic – modern and classical art intertwined with stunning high-ceilinged rooms, voluminous sofas and a maze of extraordinary bedrooms. This house can be hired for the whole weekend and I defy you not to want to stay forever. Another breathtaking beauty is Priory Hall, which can be found nestled in the Suffolk countryside. This extraordinary Tudor house and garden allows you to create an individual wedding in mesmerizing surroundings. Their main concern is that you do it your way, which is refreshing.

DECORATIONS AND ACCESSORIES

THIS section, once opened, is a veritable Pandora's Box. The possibilities for making your wedding day visually spectacular and unique are endless, and this can make the process both thrilling and daunting in equal measure. A sensible way to start is by creating a list or even a scrapbook of everything that you love and would like to somehow incorporate. You don't have to be stuck within the confines of a colour scheme unless you choose to, and actually the haphazard collection of your favourite ideas will only make your day more honest and appealing. We have been rather indoctrinated with the idea of matching themes and colours at weddings, but the time has come to throw off these shackles and have some fun.

➙ *A tiny, pressed-glass vase filled with pretty blooms is a visual delight and these look wonderful dotted down the length of a trestle table.*

Attention to Detail

Each tiny addition to your wedding celebration won't go unnoticed and adds charm and interest for guests throughout the day. Small presents, old-fashioned board games, place settings, homemade cakes, pretty straws, decorated jam jars, paper cones for flower petal confetti and paper bunting are only the start of an infinite range of possibilities. Vintage pieces and homemade projects work beautifully with these carefully considered additions, as often in the past there wouldn't have been sufficient money to fund lavish statements. It can even be fun to add a narrative to your day using props, such as old books, pictures, mirrors and other ephemera. This decorative aspect is an ideal chance to utilize the skills of family and friends, making your wedding feel very personal. You may have creative friends or a family member who loves to bake, so make use of them – it will take the pressure off you and make for great camaraderie too.

Venue Exteriors

It's worth bearing in mind that you may need to consider both the interior and exterior of your chosen venue, so we now turn to the wedding garden. Let's pretend that every wedding day has the perfect mixture of warm sun and gentle breeze – a typical hazy summer afternoon in England. You may have dreamt of having your ceremony outside or perhaps prefer to invite your guests to retire to the terrace for their first champagne saucer of fizz. Either way, this is your opportunity to create a glorious cornucopia of vintage treasures. Bunting, enamel jugs filled with wild flowers, twisted ivy, pretty lanterns, fairy lights, picnic blankets, deckchairs, vintage games – the list is endless. The wonderful thing about the garden is that you already have a perfect natural backdrop to work with. Bunting never looks better than when strung between trees and trellises. Fairy lights and lanterns come alive in the twilight, and deckchairs and blankets look at home on a manicured lawn or a pretty, overgrown field.

Bunting is the most cost effective way to make a huge impact with minimum effort. It doesn't have to be madly professional as once it's strung up in great swathes, nobody notices the intricacy of the sewing! Bunting instantly elevates the most simple and straightforward of spaces into a visual feast and it takes minutes to accomplish. The day before my wedding it had poured with rain and my heart had sunk. The following morning, only two hours prior to the ceremony, the rain finally abated and I'm sure I must have been heard feverishly hollering for miles around, 'Get the bunting up!'. It worked – our soggy garden was transformed as beautiful Liberty lawn flags fluttered as far as the eye could see.

The idea of vintage picnic blankets and deckchairs is one I have seen time and again and it never fails. Quintessentially

↑ *Seed packet bunting, fairy lights and paper lanterns, from Paperpoms.*

English and old-fashioned, it is the ideal way to bring the inside out. It's also the perfect place to flop when you have imbibed heavy quantities of champagne without securing more than a couple of scrumptious canapés! What is so lovely about this picnic-style addition to the garden is its informality. When people are lounging on the grass the atmosphere instantly takes on an effortless congeniality. There are also many lovely additions to this outdoor seating arrangement, including perhaps hiring a homemade ice cream seller or even providing guests with picnic baskets full of goodies.

Don't Buy It – Hire It

In recent years there has been an explosion of vintage hire companies on the wedding scene, which means that virtually anything is available to you – from crockery and table linen to arm chairs and moose heads! Let your imagination run riot.

There are a few hire companies that do an exceptional job. For stunning crockery, The Crockery Cupboard and Pretty Vintage have the edge. For a range of absolutely wonderful and eclectic paraphernalia, Vintage Style Hire is an absolute must. For larger items, such as trestle tables and lovely old chairs, take a look at Virginia's Vintage Hire.

Wedding Planners

There are vintage wedding planners whose skills can be employed to create every nuance and accent that you like. This allows you to avoid dreaming of where to find vintage sugar bowls and lace tablecloths for the next year. Thanks to the experience they bring, they will introduce a fountain of ideas and resources if you're feeling at a loss or a bit overwhelmed. Vintage Style Hire offer a bespoke design service to fill your day with beautiful vintage pieces and ideas.

Blogs

Since we all tend to have web access these days our gateway to another era and all its glories is tantalizingly available. We can search for hidden gems and look all over the world for them too. Ebay, Etsy and clever individuals who have set up online companies enable us to find almost anything our heart desires. Blogging has become a way to share reams of useful information, with ideas from the expert to the man on the street and the vintage wedding blogger is no exception. We wanted this book to be a tangible reference for your vintage wedding needs, but the wedding blogger has a huge contribution to make and so I have added what I consider to be the very best of them in the Where to Find section. When done well such blogs are a fantastic resource, an interesting read, a visual library and hugely inspiring.

↑ *Board games provide a great visual spectacle as vintage games had such fantastic packaging.*

↑ ↑ *A snug looking pile of picnic blankets looks so appealing and offers the perfect way to protect your guests from the evening chill.*

Games

Games are the perfect opportunity for breaking the inevitable wedding ice. There is nothing more relaxing than hearing the dull tap of a heavy wooden mallet against a croquet ball, or the sound of a gentle game of boules on gravel. Why not have a selection of favourite board games dotted about on blankets to invite guests to play? There are lots of hire companies who can provide you with all of the above and more, and it means you don't have to scour the country for everything that you would like to include. Try some of the lovely ideas that follow: they are simple, fabulous and easy to create yourself.

The Little Touches

Sometimes the addition of the simplest little things can add charm and interest to your wedding venue – try some of the following ideas, and see the next few pages for more suggestions.

↓ *Buttons and bows.*

↑ *Little glass bottles with wire place setting and flower.*

↓ *Paper cones for confetti.*

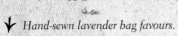
↑ *Stamped luggage label place setting.*

↓ *Hand-sewn lavender bag favours.*

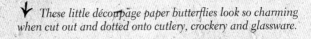
↓ *These little découpage paper butterflies look so charming when cut out and dotted onto cutlery, crockery and glassware.*

The Grand Statements

For an impressive impact think a little bigger. Grand visual gestures can be unusual, quirky or staged en masse to provide a real statement.

↓ *Simple square bunting flags in bright, plain colours. From the wedding of Emily and Ben Winn, Whitwell Hall, Norfolk.*

← *Lights galore – fairy lights, lanterns and lighting signs. From the wedding of Emi and Adam Prendergast, Blo Norton Hall, Norfolk.*

↓ *Personalized bunting, from the wedding of Tricia and Toby Nevitt, The Londesborough, London.*

How to make...

SEED PACKET BUNTING

Bunting has become a vintage wedding buzz word, but it's nice to try and do things a little differently, so why not make paper bunting rather than fabric? I found these beautiful seed packet labels and they work perfectly as bunting. Do be aware that this type of bunting is mainly for indoor use unless you are blessed with marvellous weather.

1. Decide on the string length for your bunting swag allowing for 30–40cm (12–16in) at either end for fixing purposes. I used brown garden string, but baker's twine or even ribbon will look lovely too.

Tip

You can also use vintage book illustrations, paper cut-outs or newspaper hearts.

2. Lay your string flat and at regular intervals of about 20cm (8in) use adhesive tape to secure the flags in place along the string.

3. Repeat this process but use craft glue or spray mount to fix flags to the back. This will hide the string and tape so you have a double-sided finish for each flag.

↑ *Seed packet bunting.*

How to make...

HOT CHOCOLATE IN A BAG

I love this idea. You could make lovely homemade labels for these too, or use luggage tags with a little message for your guests. Alternatively, put these ingredients for the perfect hot chocolate into little cardboard boxes or trays.

1. Fill a little paper or cellophane bag with the right amount of drinking chocolate for one person and seal it.

2. Fill another packet with mini marshmallows, a plain biscuit and a square of chocolate.

3. Put both bags into a paper cup with a striped straw or small wooden spoon and give to your guests as favours.

Tip

You could also use freshly ground coffee and chocolate-covered coffee beans for a more sophisticated gesture.

→ *Hot chocolate place setting.*

How to make...

COVERED VASES AND JAM JARS

The common jam jar can be transformed into a vintage vessel worthy of any resplendent celebration with twine, ribbon or gold leaf paint, and only requires a little effort. These look so pretty filled with one or two stems of ranunculus or craspedia. Gold leaf paint is readily available in Art and Craft shops. Instead of twine, you can use découpage scraps (available from Mamelok Papercraft) – there are lots of fantastic designs to choose from.

Using Twine

1. Cover all sides of your vase or jar with glue (I recommend E6000 Quick Hold Glue) or use double-sided adhesive tape.

2. Closely wrap the vase or jar with pretty baker's twine or gardening twine, ensuring there are no gaps. (You could also use pretty vintage lace.) Secure the first and last wrap of the twine securely so it doesn't come undone.

Using Découpage

1. Make sure your vase or jar surface is clean and dry. Paint each scrap with découpage glue and fix in place on the vase. Cover the entire surface, overlapping the scraps so there are no gaps.

2. Once the glue is completely dry, paint two or three layers of the same découpage glue over the entire surface to seal it. Spray with an acrylic sealant to finish.

Using Gold Leaf Paint

1. Ensure the surface of your vase or jam jar is clean and dry. Using a small, flat paintbrush, apply the gold leaf paint evenly onto the glass.

2. A second coat of gold leaf can be applied after 20 minutes or so if required. For a slightly different look you could use masking tape on half of the vase to leave one part as plain glass, as shown below.

↑ *Gold leaf vases with ribbon.*

THE FLOWERS

WEDDING flowers have, until fairly recently, fallen into the trap of being rather formulaic and, dare I say it, a little dull. You could even be forgiven for thinking that every florist in the country had been to the same flower arranging classes! Even as recently as my own wedding in 2009 it seemed a virtually impossible task to find a florist that could comprehend my desire for simple country flowers that weren't stuck into that Oasis product! I didn't want a bouquet trussed up with satin ribbon and forced into a tight symmetrical ball. In fact, I ended up doing the majority of the flowers myself and relied on a lovely local florist called Libby Ferris Flowers, who I finally managed to track down to make my bouquets. I wanted my flowers to look and feel as though I had wandered through an English country garden plucking pretty blooms that took my fancy.

➤ *A magnificent lace dress, with a pale pink bouquet*
in which glorious peonies take pride of place.

Say It With Flowers

Wedding flower design – or rather the lack of it – has blossomed in recent years and now it is such a relief at many weddings to see bunches of unrestrained wild flowers spilling out of French enamel jugs or pretty teapots. As far as I'm concerned nature's bounty was never meant to be trussed up and tweaked to within an inch of its life. For me, the less forced a bunch of flowers appears the more beguiling it becomes, especially at a vintage wedding.

The choice of flowers is vast these days, which means that virtually anything can be achieved. The notion of displaying flowers seems to have taken a marvellous step back in time. You can have posies in jam jars and little bottles, bouquets tied loosely with ribbon, vintage lace or garden twine and huge jugs filled with just meadow greenery. Teapots, old tins and milk bottles are just as likely to be found overflowing with country flowers as a traditional vase. The constraints of the obligatory 'wedding colour scheme' seem to have relaxed a little. Weddings with rigid colour restraints don't seem to exist in the vintage arena with such fervour as they once did, and this enables you to indulge your flower fancy in many ways and create an eclectic and diverse display. It can be so much more fun to use a mix of colour and texture in an informal way and give your reception personality and individuality.

Inspiration and Ideas

There are some simple but lovely ideas for your flower displays. For example, pretty vintage teapots with short-stemmed wild flowers or tea roses look magical. Try just one type of flower per teapot or a complete mismatch of blooms. Vary stem heights rather than arranging them in a neat ball. Fresh herbs can look wonderful mixed in with flowers and often give off a gorgeous scent, which will permeate your venue beautifully.

↑ *Flowers displays don't have to be ornate to make a statement. Little clusters of vases, potted flowers and hanging jam jars tied with ribbon and secured with baker's twine look delightful.*

↓ *A beautiful selection of wild flowers in an informal arrangement looks stunning. From the wedding of Emi and Adam Prendergast, Blo Norton Hall, Norfolk.*

Jam Jars

Jam jars are one of the unsung heroes of the vintage wedding. These look so charming just spilling over with simple hedgerow flowers, perhaps with stripy grosgrain ribbon or even ric-rac tied around their necks. I love Bonne Maman jam jars as they have such a lovely shape, so these are worth collecting if you like their strawberry jam! You could also tie a luggage tag onto these and use them as table place names too. Hanging jam jars and little bottles from tree branches and filling them with pretty flowers looks magical.

How to...

PRESERVE YOUR BOUQUET

Preserving your wedding bouquet by drying it is perfect for keeping a memento of your special day. If you don't want to keep your whole bouquet you could press just a selection of the flowers from within it.

Drying the Bouquet

1. Hang your bouquet upside down in a cool, dry, dark place, such as an airing cupboard, for about a week.

2. Once dried the bouquet will be very fragile, so store it carefully in a box, away from direct sunlight. Dry bouquets always look beautiful in vintage hat boxes lined with tissue paper.

Tip

Using silica crystals near your bouquet as it dries will speed up the drying process as the silica will absorb moisture.

Pressing Individual Flowers

1. This can be done using a flower press or you can put the flowers between greaseproof paper and in between the pages of a heavy book.

2. Once the flowers are pressed, you can present them in a beautiful vintage frame.

➤ *A hand-tied bouquet of freesias and miniature pink roses.*

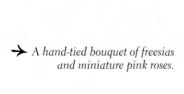

Glass Vases and Bottles

I love lots of tiny mismatched glass vases and bottles perhaps placed only 10cm (4in) apart with one or two stems in each. These not only look perfect dotted down the middle of a trestle table but also don't cause the problem of blocking the view of the proceedings or opposite guests at your table. If you find tiny glass bottles these can be filled with a single flower and used as place settings. For something a little more grandiose try tazzas, which are like cake stands only with a bowl rather than a flat surface; these look magnificent with short-stemmed blooms. Pretty Vintage hires out tazzas.

Enamel Jugs

Enamel jugs are just made for tall-stemmed blooms and these look good placed on the floor, in fireplaces, or at the ends of pews. Beautiful, tall blooms include ranunculas, anemones, irises, peonies, larkspur, delphiniums, stocks, lisianthus, hydrangeas, zinnias and even poppies. All these flowers and many more come in the most wonderful array of colours and can add a richness and depth to your floral arrangements.

If you are employing a florist it is worth writing down the flower types you really love – or you may end up with something completely unexpected. Consider scent too, noting flowers that you can't abide the smell of.

Buttonholes

Remember that an important aspect to your flower planning is the buttonholes for the menfolk – they may be small but they can still be beautiful.

↓ *Buttonholes are at their most appealing when simple and perhaps bound with raffia, ribbon or garden twine. A single craspedia or anemone can look so striking against a suit or waistcoat. Craspedia buttonholes were used in the wedding of Emily and Ben Winn, Whitwell Hall, Norfolk.*

Alternative Bouquets

One of the most important flower statements that you're going to make is with your bouquet. There are so many possibilities and as with every aspect of your vintage wedding there are always clever people pushing the traditional boundaries of what is available and acceptable.

One such alternative option is the vintage jewellery bouquet. These clever constructions are made from a large quantity of mismatched vintage brooches, earrings and buttons, which are formed into the shape of a traditional bouquet. At DC Bouquets, special pieces of jewellery or even family heirlooms can be incorporated into your exclusive bouquet design and they last forever, which is of huge appeal.

Paper bouquets have also made a fairly recent appearance and can be quite breathtaking. The level of intricacy required to make 30 or so paper blooms makes the paper bouquet something very special and unique. Again, they can be kept and even framed, and make a lovely keepsake from your wedding day. Look no further than the dexterous Suzi Mclaughlin, who constructs the most exquisite paper bouquets. She also makes paper headdresses, which can be seen in the Veils and Headdresses chapter.

↓ *Bouquet by Love Blooms, including lisianthus, hydrangea, veronica, hypericum berry, snapdragon and eucalyptus.*

How to make...
CRYSTALLIZED FRESH FLOWERS

I'm mad about crystallized flowers and they are surprisingly straightforward to make. Ensure that the flowers you choose are safe to eat, such as organic pansies, roses, marigolds, apple blossom, lavender, violets and nasturtiums. You will need: flowers, an egg white, water, fine caster (superfine) sugar, a paintbrush and a wire rack covered with greaseproof paper.

1. Remove the flowers from their stems and carefully pick off the petals. Rinse them gently, pat and leave them to dry completely.

2. Whisk the egg whites and a teaspoon of water until lightly frothy. Using a fine paintbrush, coat each petal on the top and bottom with a thin layer of the egg white mixture.

3. Dip the petals lightly into a bowl of fine caster (superfine) sugar and sprinkle sugar over the top too. Gently shake off the excess sugar.

4. Place on greaseproof paper and air dry for 12 to 24 hours. Store in an airtight container. These are the perfect addition to a wedding cake, or put them into bowls to sprinkle on desserts or to use as table decorations.

↑ *Crystallized rose petals.*

An interview with...

LOVE BLOOMS

Clare Robinson set up Love Blooms after leaving the fashion industry to train as a freelance florist. Her skill and natural ability with flowers is evident in every piece she creates. Her self-confessed style is vintage, rustic and untraditional in the best sense of the word.

. . . .

How far in advance do I need to meet with you to talk about flower ideas for my wedding?

It pays to start making initial enquiries around nine months in advance of your wedding date to be sure that the florist you want to work with is available. I would personally always email through initial ideas and quotes for you to review, to check you are happy with my ideas before arranging a face-to-face consultation. Once you meet with a florist, do ensure that you feel a connection with them and that you are confident that they understand your requirements and style.

How much does seasonality affect my choice of flowers? For example, if I love spring anemones but my wedding is in July?

With the help of greenhouses and flying flowers in from far-off lands most flowers are available all year round, but at a cost. However, if there is a type of flower you love that will be out of season and can't even be flown in on your wedding day there will usually be a beautiful alternative that can be used as a replacement and your florist will be able to advise of the available options.

◆

Are you available to look at my venue to discuss appropriate flower ideas?

Yes, I would always visit your venue before we had a final consultation to ensure all the ideas that are being suggested work within the space available. If you wanted your consultation to take place in your venue that is also possible.

Do you provide vases, jugs and jars for flower arrangements or should I source these?

I have a vast selection of vessels, ranging from glass cake stands and vintage cut-glass vases to ceramic swans and urns, which my brides are welcome to use. If you want to use something that I don't already have then I would suggest hiring it, or you may want to provide it yourself.

What is your most popular range of flowers at the moment for a vintage or rustic wedding?

The most popular flower choices for 2012 were the Memory Lane Rose, which is a gorgeous dusky lilac rose, mixed with lilac and green lisianthus, blue delphinium and lots of gorgeous foliage including herbs, arranged in a rustic 'just-picked-from-the-countryside' style. For 2013 I've had lots of multicoloured flowers in a mix of different vases and jam jars ordered. So in spring, magenta and orange ranunculus, blue anenomes, yellow craspedia and bright green foliage, such as greenbells, again mixed with herbs, will look striking and eclectic.

Roughly how much does an average wedding cost including bouquets and buttonholes?

It really does depend on your requirements. Time of year, arrangement and flower choice all have a huge impact on cost. For example, a simple hand-tied bouquet can start from £45 but if you require a bouquet brimming with more expensive blooms, such as peonies and hydrangeas, you could spend £85 or more. Table centrepieces can range from £25 for a small bouquet in a teapot or vase to £45 or more for arrangements on top of tall vases, to £95 plus for urns. Depending on how much of a presence you want your flowers to have, you could spend anything between £800 and £2,000 for a wedding of 100 people. It's possible to spend more or less than this but your florist will be able to give you an estimate based on your initial ideas. You will also have to take into account delivery and set up fees, which can be confirmed with your florist. When receiving your quote ensure it includes VAT. If it exceeds your budget ask your florist to suggest ideas to reduce costs. You will then have a clear idea about what is achievable within your budget.

THE PHOTOGRAPHY

IN some ways although your dress or shoes may have taken centre stage in this wedding extravaganza, photography is probably one of the most attention-worthy aspects of your planning. Everything you do on your wedding day, from the moment you wake full of trepidation and glee to the moment you collapse in a crumpled, emotional, satiated heap at the end of it will, hopefully, be expertly captured on film. Who you choose and how they work will be of paramount importance if you want to look back on this day with a sense of satisfaction that everything was captured perfectly.

➔ *Choosing the right photographer is crucial. From the wedding of Zoe and Richard Manders, St Albans.*

The Enduring Album

The idea of a vintage wedding photographer can seem a little unclear. It suggests sepia-tinted portraits of husbands standing stiffly behind seated wives. So let's quickly dispense with that idea and get to the crux of the matter. This is about detail, detail and more detail. Weddings, until recently, often fell into the category of what I like to describe as painting by numbers – occasions where dresses, suits, flowers and photographs virtually become indistinguishable from one another. There was often nothing to suggest a real sense of individuality or personality. For some people this is a perfectly acceptable state of affairs. However, if you're reading this book then you're probably trying to do things a little differently. So, all hail the new – and as far as I'm concerned – improved wedding photographers who have begun to emerge.

For many photographers the term vintage stems from the way the images are processed. Although the yellow tint is no longer in fashion, many still try to emulate the look and vibe of old film cameras, adding grain and so on to create images with a beautiful, timeless appeal. Armed with artistic ability and a creative eye, they're brilliantly bucking the system and are in hot demand. Close up, quirky shots with natural lighting, sun spots, interesting locations and a much more covert, unobtrusive approach means the images are meaningful and real, and often loaded with light-heartedness, intensity and raw emotion. These are the images that will endure when your memory begins to fade; those you can look at time and again to relive the magical experiences of your day, and some of the bits you missed that your photographer didn't.

➜ *Lovely blue vintage baby Diana camera. From the wedding of Tricia and Toby Nevitt.*

← *Once your photographs are taken they will be manipulated by your photographer to create beautiful, evocative images, and this is as important as the shots themselves.*

Finding the Right Photographer

To unearth the photographer who is going to do your wedding the fabulous justice it deserves, you will need to be meticulous in your search. Look through as many portfolios as you can. All of the best creative wedding photographers have websites featuring previous wedding shoots for you to pore over and you should start to get a feel of what a photographer is going to provide you with. This is not only great fun but you can also pick up fabulous tips along the way.

Photographers such as Lisa Devlin, Rosie Parsons, and our very own Jo Millington have fantastic retrospectives of recent wedding shoots and these show how they approach an event, and also the form their photos tend to take. It is worth mentioning that good photographers don't necessarily come cheap. Most wedding accoutrements are quite pricey but this is one that's worth digging a little deeper into your pocket for. We don't seem to have much trouble spending thousands of pounds on a wedding dress, but baulk at spending the same on a wedding photographer. The thing is that you truly do get what you pay for and you will have your wedding album long after the day begins to fade in your mind's eye. What you pay for is that perfect combination of technical and artistic ability. This deftness and intuitive skill of the professional photographer is the way to capture those magical shots, and it's no mean feat, so when you come across the right one 'snap them up'.

Photo Booths

This is good old-fashioned, silly fun in a dressing-up box – think props and a cleverly constructed stage or jolly backdrop. Some wedding photographers offer a photo booth as an extra service. It can be anything from a 1950s airstream caravan courtesy of The Photo Emporium, to a portable photography studio from Cotton Candy Photography. This is also something you can orchestrate yourself with a backdrop sheet and a healthy dose of imagination. Silly props are a useful extra, including signage, moustaches, hats, glasses and fake noses. You don't need to man it as you can have a remote shutter on the camera and a sturdy tripod. Photo booths are a fabulous way for guests to really let their hair down, and also mean that you have a whole separate selection of photos whilst your photographer is busy elsewhere.

Cine Film

Many recent vintage-style weddings have seen the re-emergence of the cine camera. Films recorded on Super 8 have become immensely fashionable and the result, if done properly, is a retrospective of your day that looks and feels truly vintage and marvellous. Mark Brown is one such talent and can turn your wedding day into what feels like an outtake from *Roman Holiday*. Price-wise this is quite an expensive option, but if you get a beautiful handmade film out of it that lasts until eternity then I for one think it's worth it.

An interview with...

JOANNA MILLINGTON
PHOTOGRAPHY

Jo Millington has been professionally shooting weddings for a number of years and as if you didn't have proof enough of her talents from her beautiful website and blog, she also took every stunning shot in this book.

How far in advance should I book a photographer?

There are no hard and fast rules, but the majority of my couples book me a year in advance. However, I have taken a booking as little as two weeks before the wedding day! The closer you leave it, the bigger gamble you are taking that the photographer won't be free.

What should I look for when deciding on the right photographer?

I really do believe photography today is an art form and each wedding photographer has their own unique style. Browse as many wedding blogs and photographer sites as possible. Many photographers tend to attract a certain kind of couple, so look for weddings similar to yours. If you look at someone else's wedding photos and wish they were your own then you've probably found the photographer for you.

What can I expect from a good photographer prior to and during my event?

Peace of mind. You should feel that the photographer has it covered and you have very little to think about. A good photographer will ask all the right questions. You should definitely have a consultation as part of your package, so that on your wedding day they will get on with their job and you can get on with your day. On the day they should be both invisible but able to take control when needed, for example during the formal shots and portrait sessions. They should make you and all your guests feel comfortable, and should be there for you. Don't be afraid to ask them if you want a picture of you and your Nan on the dance floor!

How can I get the best out of my photographer?

Strike up a rapport with your photographer: think of them as a working guest. Tell them as much about you and your wedding as possible. I do become good friends with some of my clients. Keep the photographer informed of your schedule as much as possible so that they can ensure they're in the right place at the right time. Very importantly, think about your timings. For example, will it be getting dark at the time of the service? Ask your photographer how long it will take for the formal shots and how many they recommend you have. Give plenty of time for a good portrait session. The more you give your photographer the more you'll get out of it, so do ask them anything. This is probably the first wedding you've planned, whereas they've been a central part of around a hundred.

As a wedding photographer, what advice would you give when planning our day?

Think about the time of day, time of year and amount of daylight. Natural daylight always makes for the most flattering photography. Take this into account when choosing the time for your ceremony and allowing time for the portraits and formals. This is the biggest and most important party you'll ever throw. Don't do what you think you should do, do what you want to do and how you want to do it. In my experience these always make for the best weddings and the happiest ever-after couples.

How many photographs can I expect to receive? And will I receive an album and disc too?

Always ask your photographer how many images you can expect, but I would suggest between 500–700 images. You should always receive a disc. Some photographers include albums as part of their package. Many, myself included, provide them as an extra, but always check first.

Will you take specific photographs for me or is the choice of image left up to you?

Other than formals and portraits most photographers tend to just shoot the day as it naturally progresses. I always make sure I get detail shots, decor, place settings, venue, cake and so on. I try to get as many guests as possible, though I can never guarantee I will get everyone. If you have specific shots you would like, it is very important to inform your photographer of this before the day so that they can make a note of it.

THE CAKE

IT may be slightly unorthodox to start this chapter by discussing the merits of a virtually naked wedding cake, particularly in light of the fact that I adore eating the icing on cakes, but these simply adorned offerings are, quite frankly, irresistible. Freshly baked, light as a feather sponge cakes in their most basic form, presented with little more than a dusting of icing sugar and thick layers of butter icing somehow become tantalizingly reminiscent of dolls' house food and children's stories. Wedding cakes have always been an opportunity to create something resplendent and intricately decorated but these deconstructed, slightly rustic cakes give them a run for their money, and fit so perfectly into any wedding, be it vintage or modern. They also look wonderful adorned with pretty fresh flowers or crystallized petals, which incidentally are available from Eat My Flowers.

➤ *Fabulous catering company Cooper and Read will produce the ultimate flower-adorned tower for you.*

↑ *A perfect example of an elegant and delicate-looking wedding cake. From the wedding of Joanna and Dave Adkins, The Londesborough, London.*

The Icingless Cake

Cooper and Read create beautiful flower-adorned towers, but if you are feeling brave and love baking this could be one to attempt yourself, and you don't need a skilled professional to ice or finish it. Quite frankly, the more wobbly and homemade looking the better.

The Traditional Tiered Cake

The tiered wedding cake has a fascinating heritage. In its original form this celebratory cake took the shape of a tower, where biscuits, pies and scones were piled high into a mound. The bride and groom were then challenged to kiss over the top, and if they managed to do so without upsetting the precariously balanced morsels then a lifetime of happiness and prosperity was assured (a bit grim if the tower did fall over though!). Since then the wedding cake has been through many guises and today anything is possible, but in many ways the time-honoured spectacle of exemplary piping and ribbon on a tiered cake is an opportunity not to be overlooked. Sometimes tradition is a wonderful thing to break and yet other times it can be a chance to recognize the passage of time and the passing on of unique rituals that have continued for generations.

Alternative Wedding Cakes

The Pork Pie

One could be forgiven for thinking that a pork pie as a wedding cake is a crazy modern invention, but not so. In the 17th century there was a tradition for 'bride pie', which was often savoury and included ingredients such as oysters, mutton, mace and chestnuts. The brilliant thing about a savoury offering is that it can be eaten later in the evening post-dancing when your guests tend to become a ravenous gaggle. Companies such as Brays Cottage Pork Pies and Adams and Harlow create wonderful, hot water crust pork pies that look fabulously wonky and homemade – perfect for a big vintage country wedding in the garden.

The Cheese Cake

Another sight to behold that is fast becoming a familiar alternative to the traditional wedding cake is a magnificent and mouth-watering tiered stack of whole cheeses. Imagine a simple barn wedding with hay bales, picnic rugs, vintage tablecloths on trestle tables stuffed with delicious homemade goodies, and at its epicentre a pile of wonderful cheese. Experts in the field of fromage can give advice on the best cheeses for stacking, for example The Fine Cheese Company or The Cheese Shed. This makes a scrumptious and unusual looking centrepiece, which again can be added to your evening buffet for hungry revellers. And might I suggest a delicious accompaniment of homemade chutney and crusty bread to make this a truly homespun and rustic extravaganza.

Vintage as a word has become so broadly used, but to be accurate if you love all things vintage then history has to play its part. One company that excels in exquisite cakes is Amy Swann Cakes, offering an unfaltering wonderful selection. She will create mood boards for your confection to ensure that the cake is original and perfectly to your taste.

The Little Cupcake

Having been so vocal about my love of the long-established, tiered wedding cake, I also have huge affection for the humble cupcake – and who doesn't? The thing about a cupcake is that it sits so beautifully atop a vintage cake stand and so a match is made in heaven. The sight of beautiful cakes piled high on delicate china is a thing of beauty to behold. It also dispenses with the problem of some poor soul in the kitchen portioning up your wedding cake.

I feel that the most charming aspect of these little morsels is their imperfection. I'm not a fan of absolutely immaculate cupcakes that look as though they have come straight off the nearest production line. I prefer this feast for the eyes and tummy to have boundless natural charm and look like it has been lovingly baked and decorated, even if there is the odd flaw. Actually, this is one of those jobs that you can delegate to a friend or family member, which makes it so wonderfully personal. However, if deftness in the kitchen is in short supply there are some lovely companies that will do the honours for you. The Primrose Bakery in London is one such deft and delightful company and there are many others who will whip up truly magnificent cupcakes for your wedding day – see the Where to Find section.

→ *These exquisite offerings from The Queen of Hearts Cookies Company would make excellent favours or gifts for your guests.*

Individual Cookies

Speaking of an individual morsel for each guest rather than a whole cake, then these hand-baked treasures may appeal. It's always very thrilling to unearth something new and expertly done that sets your heart aflutter, and this company does that very thing. The Queen of Hearts Cookies Company creates charming and delicious cookies embellished with decorations, such as gold-tinted roses and pretty lattice work, which literally look too good to eat.

How to make...
A CAKE TOPPER

Cake toppers are currently having their moment, but let me be clear that I'm not referring to the little figures that traditionally stand atop your cake. I'm much more excited about the pint-sized bunting-type messages as shown here. They add a whimsical, decorative touch and can be a lovely addition to a simply designed cake. It's possible to commission beautiful ones from an expert in the field of cake toppers, such as Kate Seaward at I Like Pens. She designs and creates bespoke pieces that are so delightful, as shown here. It's also very easy to make your own charming cake topper. You will need: dowelling, twine or string, pretty paper for flags, glue and scissors.

1. The cake topper shown below was made with two vintage knitting needles as the flagpoles. Start by knotting baker's twine to the knitting needles.

2. Cut out double-sided flags, stamped with a word of your choosing, for example, LOVE.

3. Fold each flag over the twice and use glue to seal each flag together at the bottom – quick, yet effective.

Tip

Instead of using knitting needles as flagpoles on your cake topper you could use straws, thin lengths of wood dowelling or wooden skewers.

↑ *This homemade cake topper was constructed using pretty paper, a stamp kit, some baker's twine and a pair of lovely knitting needles.*

← *Fantastic cake topper from I Like Pens, which sets off this homemade cake to perfection. From the wedding of Hayley and Neil Gosling, The Plough, Norwich.*

MUSIC AND DANCING

FANTASTIC – it's the dancing bit! On my wedding day I had no intention of uttering a syllable before a seated room of over a hundred friends and family. However, upon realizing that these were all the most important people in my life, and fuelled by more than a few glasses of fizz, I felt the need to leap to my feet and holler, 'I can't wait to dance with you all!' And it was true. During our ceremony we had decided on a lone cellist to accompany us down the aisle. I am always so moved by a single skilful musician filling the space with beautiful sound. If this style of accompaniment to your day appeals then a classical acoustic musician called My Guitarist is well worth investigating further. However, the bit I was really looking forward to at our wedding was the brilliant French DJ who rocked our party until the wee small hours.

→ *A beautiful, atmospheric scene from the wedding of Emily and Rob Flatt, East Anglian Railway Museum, Colchester.*

Put on Your Dancing Shoes

With the serious business of your wedding vows fading blissfully with the daylight, this is the time to really celebrate and there are a plethora of possibilities. Just because you opt for a 1920s dress it doesn't mean you have to Charleston the night away. My advice is to choose the music that you love but also consider what will entice your guests on to the dance floor. The evening party we had was the most memorable part of our day because I felt relaxed and free of responsibility. However, it would have felt a little lacklustre if I was the only one on the dance floor, so be mindful of what will whip your wedding throng into a dancing frenzy.

↑ Bride and groom get into the dancing mood. From the wedding of Kelly and James Alcock, Braziers Park, Reading.

← Having such fun! From the wedding of Helen and James Renwick, MC Motors, London.

There is a musical feast of vintage possibilities. Close harmony singers, such as The Spinettes and The Victory Dolls, bring more than a touch of wartime glamour to your event. There are barber shop quartets, skiffle bands and DJs who specialize in 45 records played on original gramophones, such as The Vintage DJ or The Shellac Sisters. There are also fabulous DJs that mix brilliant contemporary music with retro tunes, such as US-based company, Flashdance, or DJs that care about what they choose and who it's for, such as DJ Heather Thompson. And if you want your wedding to go with a vintage swing then look no further than Down For The Count, The Little Big Band or Goose Bumps Music.

↑ *Making the band and the music personal to you will make the event more memorable. From the wedding of Kelly and James Alcock, Braziers Park, Reading.*

→ *Weddings are a time for everyone to get on the dance floor. From the wedding of Helen and James Renwick, MC Motors, London.*

FINISHING TOUCHES

IT'S hard to know where to start with this chapter, but there are a few dazzling ideas that I've come across that seem to stand head and shoulders above the rest. Whether it is a den-making area for the children or a do-it-yourself ice cream parlour, it's these thoughtful and unusual additions that ensure that your event is memorable and truly personal. Some of the following suggestions are easy to create yourself and others are items that can be hired. All are stupendous, great fun and will have your guests jumping for joy and talking about your wedding day long after it is over.

→ *This vintage wooden cutlery drawer is filled with delicious extras for decorating ice creams – who wouldn't be tempted?*

↑ *Homemade
fudge looks
fantastic wrapped
with red ribbon.*

← *A large glass
bonbon dish topped
with coconut-covered
marshmallows and
a charming cake
topper by I Like Pens.*

↓ *Homemade
jigsaw-shaped
biscuits.*

Pudding or Sweetie Table

The pudding table is a wonderful idea for getting friends and family involved. Baking for a wedding day is such a warm-hearted way to show your affection, so nobody would dream of turning you down, even if their steamed treacle sponge does lack a little finesse. There are fabulous hire companies who can provide you with tiered cake stands, platters and bowls for every size and shape of pudding or cake. You can embellish with signage, pretty tablecloths, vintage china and fabric napkins and your guests can just keep going back for more! Of course if you don't want to risk Aunty May's lacklustre Victoria sandwich sponge there are plenty of catering companies that will provide you with a cake and pudding array fit for a king. Cooper and Read is one clever outfit that will whip up a pudding table to satiate any sweet-toothed wedding guest.

Alternatively, fill jars and bowls with the sweets we all know and love – who can turn down a sherbert pip or pear drop? You can also write wonderfully jolly descriptions on luggage labels. Include candy striped paper bags and some vintage weighing scales for extra charm. You could even make homemade sweets and package them up individually.

Ice Cream Table

Equally appropriate for the sybarite in all of us is the Ice Cream Parlour. You can hire an ice cream van, tricycle or even a company serving ices from a split-screen camper van, pop them somewhere on the grass and watch the hordes gather. Alternatively, hire company Pretty Vintage will provide everything you need to set up your own vintage-style ice cream parlour table, including scoops, signage, tablecloth, paper ice cream tubs, napkins and bowls. The only thing you need to do is provide the ice cream and edible extras – think of pretty pots and sundae glasses filled to the brim with sprinkles, sauces, mini meringues, marshmallows, chocolate flakes; anything to attract a sweet tooth – and you have an ice cream feast fit for a king!

↑ ← Glassware and striped paper ice cream tubs supplied by Pretty Vintage and filled with all sorts of delicious ice cream toppings.

← Why not hire your own ice cream seller?

Message Table

Asking your guests to leave a message for you on your wedding day is like filling in that holiday visitor's book. Guests love reading what everyone else has written and it can be a poignant, moving and humorous reminder of your day.

A clever idea is to install a vintage typewriter (which can be hired from a number of vintage hire companies) on a pretty little table or desk. Provide beautiful paper or postcards and envelopes, a pinboard or even a set of hooks and ask your guests to type a message. You could also provide a hole punch and pretty ribbon or string so that the note can be tied onto a tree or branch. If you want the messages to be secret then a little postbox or suitcase can be a lovely idea too. There are so many ways to incorporate this message idea and it's a perfect addition to your wedding scrapbook.

↑ *Vintage typewriters are relatively easy to find, but make sure they are in good working order and replace the old ribbon if necessary. From the wedding of Tricia and Toby Nevitt, The Londesborough, London.*

Suitcase Seating Plan

Table seating plans can often cause headaches, and getting them just right can take a lot of time and thought, but once you have decided who is sitting next to who, there are some charming and unusual ways to display your seating arrangements. One inventive possibility is to use an open suitcase to peg your lists inside. Alternatively, you could use an old easel with a picture frame hung with manila luggage labels. Even lists pegged to a washing line can look fun, especially if you're eating outside.

← *An old suitcase creates a perfect vintage touch, especially when used to display seating arrangements.*

Children's Fun

Now this really is a jolly bit to organize. It's a bit of light relief to plan a den-making area with blankets and chairs, or an art table full of exciting bits for sticking and gluing. What about crown or mask making and decorating, a face painting table, a dressing-up box or even a personalized activity pack full of fun things to keep your little guests entertained? This could include a matchbox, which they have to fill with ten tiny finds, or a little treasure hunt with a map. If you have a lovely garden and a sunny day then even races and hide and seek can be great fun.

Many of these ideas don't need to cost a fortune. Depending on how many children there are, it can be worth employing somebody to solely oversee the children, or enlist the help of the older ones to look after the younger ones. You can also hire a great selection of games that will appeal to adults and children alike – everything from croquet, boules, quoits, twister and ping-pong (see details of hire companies listed in Where to Find at the back of the book).

← ↑ A bag of goodies is such a great idea for your little guests and will keep them entertained, especially during the wedding breakfast. Both images from the wedding of Tricia and Toby Nevitt, The Londesborough, London.

REAL WEDDINGS INSPIRATION

IT is easy and hugely enjoyable for me to wax lyrical about the multitude of ways in which you can add vintage touches to your wedding day, but what I really want to show you is how it can and has been done. This section is a sweetie shop of wedding photographs for you to pour over. The following couples have expertly mixed vintage with their very own personal nuances to make these wedding celebrations look effortlessly stylish, individual and totally captivating. I hope that some of the images give you huge inspiration and the courage to do exactly what you want, even if it is to sit your guests on park benches or invite them to dance around a maypole and drink through stripy straws. It may not be what your Mother or Grandmother approves of but then, it's not their day!

→ *The wedding of Christina Rich and Derek Morris (my parents) in 1963.*

↑ ↓ *The wedding of Jo and Dan.*
Photographed by Lee Robbins Photographic.

↑ ↓ *The wedding of Emi and Adam.*
Photographed by Joanna Millington.

↑ *The wedding of Joey and Mike.*
Photographed by Lisa Jane Photography.

↑ *The wedding of Hels and Lewis.*
Photographed by Laura Mccluskey Photography.

↓ *The wedding of Jo and Dan.*
Photographed by Lee Robbins Photographic.

WHERE TO FIND

This section is intended to provide you with a resource to help you hunt out those vintage details that make all the difference.

Dresses

www.atelier-mayer.com
www.basia-zarzycka.com
www.lovemissdaisy.com
www.net-a-porter.com
www.charliebrear.com
www.poshgirlvintage.com
www.halfpennylondon.com
www.elizabethavey.co.uk
www.thefrock.com
www.julietpoyser.co.uk
www.vintagedress.co.uk
www.janebourvis.co.uk
www.furcoatnoknickers.co.uk
www.circabrides.com
www.heirloomcouture.com
www.abigailsvintagebridal.co.uk
www.oohlalavintage.com
www.hopeandharlequin.com
www.primvintagefashion.com
www.heavenlyvintagebrides.co.uk
www.daughtersofsimone.com
www.minna.co.uk
www.melamela.co.uk
www.belleandbunty.co.uk
www.ditaflorita.com
www.zoelem.co.uk
www.annebarclay.com
www.twigsandhoney.com
www.joanneflemingdesign.com
www.clairepettibone.com
www.froufroubride.co.uk
www.vintagedeli.co.uk
www.charlottecasadejus.com
www.anniesvintageclothing.co.uk

Wedding Fairs

www.amostcurious
weddingfair.co.uk
www.missvintageaffair.co.uk

Alteration Companies

www.bridalalterations.co.uk
www.splendidstitches.co.uk
www.abigailsvintagebridal.co.uk
www.resurrectionboutique.co.uk
www.paperdressvintage.co.uk

Specialist Cleaning Companies

www.mayflowercleaners.co.uk
www.themastercleaners.com
www.pdem.co.uk
www.heritagegown.com

Lingerie

www.lucileandco.com
www.kissmedeadly.co.uk
www.whatkatiedid.com
www.stockingsandromance.co.uk
www.rigbyandpeller.com
www.agentprovocateur.co.uk
www.luellasboudoir.co.uk
www.lovebysusie.co.uk
www.clairepettibone.com
www.rosy.fr
www.aytengasson.com
www.playfulpromises.com
www.thisismuuna.tumblr.com

Shoes

www.emmyshoes.co.uk
www.shoesofprey.com
www.hettyrose.co.uk
www.luellasboudoir.co.uk
www.rainbowclub.co.uk
(featuring shoes by Diane Hassall)
www.figgieshoes.com
www.riceandbeansvintage.com
www.absolutevintage.co.uk
www.queensandbowl.com
www.rachelsimpsonshoes.com
www.harrietwilde.com
www.shopbando.com
www.vintageheaddresses.com
www.absolutelyaudrey.com
www.myglassslipper.com
www.nickyrox.co.uk
www.pourlavictoire.com
www.remixvintageshoes.com
www.girlsofelegance.co.uk

Veils and Headdresses

www.honitonlace.com
www.antiquelaceheirlooms.com
www.etsy.com/shop/
TheHouseOfKatSwank
www.pearlsandswine.com
www.bethmorgan.co.uk

www.baba-c.co.uk
www.janetaylormillinery.com
www.piphackett.co.uk
www.sheenaholland.com
www.williamchambers.co.uk
www.twigsandhoney.com
www.etsy.com/shop/TessaKim
www.birdcageveils.com
www.unveiledbridaldesigns.com
www.dream-veils.co.uk
www.vintageheaddresses.co.uk
www.byharriet.co.uk
www.annelliclarke.com
www.lovebysusie.co.uk
www.dollsandlace.com
www.garlandsofgrace.com
www.thevintagebride.com
www.suzimclaughlin.
blogspot.co.uk
www.ladameauberet.com
www.hollyyoungboutique.com
www.jochristoforides.co.uk
(bespoke veils)
www.jobarnesvintage.com
Edwina Ibbotson Shop at 45
Queenstown Road, Battersea,
London SW8 3RG (no website)

Hair

www.powderroom.org.uk
www.flamingoamy.co.uk
www.vintagehairlounge.com
www.ninashairparlour.com
www.vintage-styling.com
www.missdixiebelle.co.uk
www.itssomethinghells.com
www.decodolls.co.uk

Make-up

www.thevintagecosmetic
company.co.uk
www.lovemoimakeup.com
www.sabrinalily.co.uk
www.bethanyjanedavies.co.uk
www.danirichardson.co.uk
www.thepowderpuffgirls.com

Jewellery

www.vintagebridaljewellery.co.uk
www.magpievintage.co.uk
www.victoriamillesime.co.uk
www.katherineswaine.co.uk
www.laurel-lime.co.uk

www.jobarnesvintage.com
www.lottielovesvintage.co.uk
www.furcoatnoknickers.co.uk
www.rosieweisencrantz.com
www.eclecticeccentricity.co.uk
www.renewalrus.co.uk
www.paleandinteresting.com
www.glitzysecrets.com
www.bejewelledvintage.co.uk
www.the-little-things-in-life.co.uk
www.vintagestyler.co.uk
www.floandpercy.com
www.libertyinlove.co.uk
www.karinandreasson
jewellery.com
www.vintageseekers.com
www.gillianmillion.com
www.vintagejewellery.co.uk

Grooms

www.vintageswank.com
www.absolutevintage.co.uk
www.savvyrow.co.uk
www.vivienofholloway.com
www.hornetskensington.co.uk
www.vintagetovoguebath.co.uk
www.classicchaps.co.uk
www.therealmccoy.co.uk
www.old-town.co.uk
www.tweedmansvintage.co.uk
www.gentlemansemporium.com
www.victorvalentine.co.uk

Bridesmaids

Adults
www.zoelem.co.uk
www.melamela.co.uk
www.abigailsvintagebridal.co.uk
www.sewdirect.com
www.deargolden.blogspot.co.uk
www.minna.co.uk
www.annebarclay.com

Children
www.myaddiesattic.com
www.bluebelleandco.com
www.ilovegorgeous.co.uk
www.littlelinens.co.uk
www.cherubchild.com
www.bonpoint.com
www.luluandflo.co.uk
www.edensbouquet.com
www.facebook.com/BestOfYouth

Stationery

www.leafcutterdesigns.com
www.abigailwarner.com
www.artcadia.co.uk
www.berinmade.com
www.razzledazzlerose.co.uk
www.story-house.co.uk
www.hellolucky.co.uk
www.somethingkindacute.com
www.alicegabb.com
www.dottiecreations.com
www.goldenappledesigns.co.uk
www.weddinginateacup.co.uk
www.ilikepens.co.uk
www.strawberrysorbet.co.uk
www.emmajo.co.uk
www.bellafigura.com
www.lucyjanebatchelor.co.uk
www.charliescribble.com
www.hollyhocklane.co.uk
www.vintage-designs.co.uk
www.veronicadearly.com
www.yieldink.co.uk
www.birdandbanner.com
www.wolfwhistlestudio.co.uk
www.alison-russell.co.uk
www.printablepress.com
www.lovevsdesign.com

Wedding Blogs/Websites

www.rockmywedding.co.uk
www.whimsicalwonderland
weddings.com
www.greenweddingshoes.com
www.ruffledblog.com
www.stylemepretty.com
www.rocknrollbride.com
www.london-bride.com
www.bleubirdvintage.
typepad.com
www.lucysaysido.co.uk
www.thenaturalwedding
company.co.uk

Wedding Planners

www.jollygoodwedding.com
www.vintagestylehire.co.uk

Locations

www.manningtongardens.co.uk
(Medieval manor, Norfolk)
www.tintabernacle.com
(Tin chapel, East Sussex)
www.steppingbeyond.co.uk
(Walking wedding, Herefordshire)
www.castlegibson.com/locations/
mc-motors (Warehouse, London)

www.polhawnfort.com
(Fort on Cornish cliffs)
www.wiseweddingvenue.co.uk
(Outdoor wedding venue, Kent)
www.clavelshaybarn.co.uk
(Farm, Somerset)
www.cowparsleyweddings.com
(Farm, Somerset)
www.cleywindmill.co.uk
(Windmill, Norfolk)
www.voewood.com (Arts and
Crafts country house, Norfolk)
www.inshriachhouse.com
(Scotland)
www.swallowtailhill.com
(Farm, East Sussex)
www.thechichesterhall.org.uk
(Village hall, Surrey)
www.barrington-park.co.uk
(Village hall, Oxfordshire)
www.prioryhall.com
(Tudor Hall, Suffolk)
www.bruisyardhall.co.uk
(13th century hall, Suffolk)
www.horsebridgestation.co.uk
(Railway station, Hampshire)
www.thekeeperandthedell.com
(Dell, Norfolk)

Marquees

www.vintagemarquees.co.uk
www.funkymonkeytents.co.uk

Decorations and Accessories

www.pompomstudio.co.uk
www.paperpoms.co.uk
www.sunbeamjackie.com
www.virginiasvintagehire.co.uk
www.prettyvintage.co.uk
www.lavenderandlinen.co.uk
www.thecrockerycupboard.co.uk
www.uksignwarehouse.com
www.bonbonballoons.com
www.vowedandamazed.co.uk
www.papermash.co.uk
www.mamelok.com

Flowers

www.foragefor.co.uk
www.realflowers.co.uk
www.freedomflowers.co.uk
www.blush-floral-design.com
www.suzimclaughlin.
blogspot.co.uk
www.loveblooms.co.uk
www.misspickering.blogspot.com
www.jenniflower.co.uk
www.dcbouquets.co.uk

www.broochbouquets.com
www.libbyferrisflowers.co.uk
www.cutflowergarden.co.uk
www.philippacraddock.co.uk

Photography

www.alvinburrows.com
www.lauramccluskey
photography.com
www.lisajane-photography.com
www.abicampbell
photography.com
www.joannamillington
photography.com
www.jenniehill.com
www.kat-hill.com
www.mark-tattersall.co.uk
www.ourblogoflove.com
www.thelittlecaravan.co.uk
www.rosieparsons.com
www.devlinphotos.co.uk
www.robbinsphotographic.com
www.wenotmecollective.com
www.emmacasephotography.com
www.cottoncandyweddings.co.uk
www.philippajames
photography.com
www.thephotoemporium.com
www.markbrown
photography.co.uk

Super 8mm Films

www.chestnutproductions.com
www.markwbrown.com
www.thesundaysaloon.com
www.hellosuper8.com

Cakes

www.queenofheartscookie
company.co.uk
www.utterlysexycafe.co.uk
www.amyswanncakes.co.uk
www.eatmyflowers.co.uk
www.verysweetdesserts.com
www.laelcakes.com
www.zoeclarkcakes.com
www.cakehero.com
www.vanillaparlour.co.uk
www.frenchmade.co.uk
www.cooperandread.co.uk
www.rosalindmillercakes.com
www.perfectpie.co.uk
www.adamsandharlow.co.uk
www.finecheese.co.uk
www.thecheeseshed.com

Cupcakes

www.cupcakeslondon.com
www.chattercakes.co.uk
www.georgetowncupcake.com
www.swallowbakery.co.uk
www.primrose-bakery.co.uk
www.mscupcake.co.uk
www.crumbs.com
www.magnoliabakery.com

Music and Dancing

www.theflashdance.com
www.vintagedj.com
www.shellacsisters.co.uk
www.thevictorydolls.tumblr.com
www.thespinettes.co.uk
www.get-knotted.net (duke box)
www.myguitarist.co.uk
www.mr-tunes-vintage-dj.co.uk
www.djheatherthompson.com
www.downforthecount.co.uk
www.littlebigbandmusic.co.uk
www.goosebumpsmusic.co.uk

Finishing Touches

www.the-tea-set.co.uk
www.dishandspoonfood.co.uk
www.thesilverapples.com
www.misstea.co.uk
www.prettyvintage.co.uk
www.vintageenglish.co.uk
www.icecreamtrikebike.co.uk
www.the-tea-set.co.uk
www.kissmycake.co.uk
www.splitscreenicecream.com
www.vintagescoops.co.uk
www.icebaby.co.uk
www.thevintageweddinglist.co.uk
www.cooperandread.co.uk

ACKNOWLEDGMENTS

When I started writing this book nearly two years ago I don't think I allowed myself to imagine it would ever be published. However, through some old-fashioned slog, much mirth, the fabulous chance meeting of the talented photographer Jo Millington and the vision and utter professionalism of Jane Mann of Penrose Publishing Services, we have managed it, and I am incredibly proud of it.

There were an enormous amount of clever, gorgeous and supportive people involved in so many aspects of this book. Huge and heartfelt thanks are owed to all the individuals and companies listed below. This also extends to my husband Kevin and three miraculous children, Ottilie, Rufus and Agatha, who have let me hide away writing and researching for hours on end with only miniscule amounts of grumbling.

Locations – Simon Finch at Voewood House, Lady Walpole at Mannington Hall, Constance Thompson at The End House, Lauren at The Sir Garnet.

Clothing, Shoes, Jewellery and Accessories – Simeon Morris at Simeon C, James and Shona at Prim Vintage, Katy Coe at Vintage Deli, Jonny at Elements, Marie and Will at Old Town, Imelda's Shoes, Lucy Crick at Eclectic Eccentricity, Suzi Mclaughlin, Christina Morris, Garlands of Grace, Juliet at Paperpoms UK.

Millinery – Annelli Clarke at Annelli Clarke.

Make-up – Emily at Love Moi Make-up, Nova at Milk and Honey, Amy Taylor at Flamingo Amy.

Hair – Amy Taylor at Flamingo Amy, Susan at The Cutting Crew.

Stationery – Kate Seaward at I Like Pens, Andrew and Sarah at Strawberry Sorbet, Flo at Charlie Scribble, Brooke Woolley at Wolf Whistle.

Cakes – Ruth and Kate at Cooper and Read.

Models – Charlie Crampton, Laila Patteson, Faye Tattam, Ellen Burton, Jude Wright, Sarah Henman, Gemma Dietrich, Tessa Killingbeck, Summer Clover, Paul Flack, Lois Millington Flack, Kate McCaul, Hannah Campbell, Catherine Edgeley.

Shoot Styling – Abigail Morris, Nicky Barrell.

Flowers – Clare Robinson at Love Blooms.

Expert Interviews – Louise Hill at Hope and Harlequin, Amy Taylor at Flamingo Amy, Katie Reynolds at The Powderpuff Girls, Abigail Haughton at Abigail's Vintage Bridal, Katie Thomas at What Katie Did, Henrietta Rose Samuels at Hetty Rose Limited, Susie McKenzie at LovebySusie, Emma Prescott at Emma Jo, Clare Robinson at Love Blooms, Joanna Millington at Joanna Millington Photography.

Drawings – Christina Morris.

Photography – Joanna Millington Photography, Lisa Jane Photography, Laura Mccluskey Photography, Robbins Photographic.

ABOUT THE AUTHOR

Lucy initially trained as a Fine Art Painter and has a long-standing interest in visual style and aesthetics in all aspects of her daily life. She is now the mother of three children, Ottilie aged 7, Rufus aged 5 and Agatha aged 3. Following her own vintage-inspired wedding in 2009 she set up a vintage crockery hire company, Pretty Vintage, enabling her to work from home, to indulge her passion for vintage finds and make use of her creativity. Pretty Vintage blossomed into a successful business and gave Lucy huge insight into the wedding industry. Her wealth of knowledge particularly pertaining to vintage-style weddings has been coupled with a love of writing to produce *The Complete Vintage Wedding Guide*.

INDEX

Note: Page numbers in **bold** refer to information contained in captions.

1920s
    clothing **11**, 30, 32
    jewellery 8, **68**, 70, **70**
    make-up **62**, 64
1930s
    clothing 15, 23, **27**, 40, 41, 55, 76
    hair **50**, **53**, 58, 59
    jewellery 68, 70, **70**
    make-up 62
1940s
    clothing **3**, 8, **11**, 24, 40–1, 65, **81**
    hair **52**, **54**, 58, 59
    jewellery 70–1, **70**
    make-up **62**, 64
1950s
    clothing **3**, 8, **11**, 15, 26, 41, **41**, 79
    hair 58
    jewellery 70–1
    make-up **63**, 64
1960s
    clothing **10**, **11**, 21, 23, **32**, 41, **134**
    jewellery 71, **71**
    make-up 63
1970s
    clothing 8, **8**, **13**, 17, 50, 76
    jewellery 71
    make-up 63

Abigail's Vintage Bridal 13–15, 78

Bakelite jewellery 70–1, **70**
blogs 97
bridesmaids 76–81, **76**, **78–9**
bunting 96, **96**, **100**, 101, **101**

cakes 118–23, **118**, **120–1**, 136
    cheese cakes 121
    icingless **118**, 120
    pork pie 121
    toppers 123, **123**, 130
    traditional 120, **120**
children 97, **97**, 133, **133**
    see also flower girls
cine film 115
confetti holders 98

cookies 120, 121, **130**
cupcakes 121, **121**

dancing 124–7, **124**, **126–7**
decorations and accessories 94–103, **94**, **96–103**
    games 97, **97**
    grand statements 100, **100**
    hiring 96–7
    location exteriors 96
    place settings 98–9, 102, **102**
    table touches 98, **98–9**, 102, **102**
    see also flowers
dresses **3–4**, 7–8, **8–23**, **10**, **13**, **16–19**, **21**, **50**, **55**, **75**, **134**, **138**
    alterations 13–15, 20–2
    and body shape 16
    bridesmaid 76, **78–9**, **81**
    finding 16–17, 22–3
    and hairstyles 59
    made-to-order 20
    and make-up 65
    odour removal 21
    stain removal 21
    styles **11**
    and underwear 29
    and veils 49
    vintage-inspired 18
    washing 19, 21

Emma Jo 84, 86–7

favours 99, **120**
finishing touches 128–33, **128**, **130–3**
Flamingo Amy 53, 58–9
flower girls 76, 81, **81**
flowers 104–111, **104**, **106–9**
    alternative 108
    bouquets **4**, **53**, 104, **104**, 107–8, **107–8**, 111, **138**
    buttonholes 108, **108**, 136
    crystallized 109, **109**
    enamel jugs 108
    jam jars 103, **103**, 106, **106**
    paper 108
    preserving 107, **107**
    table 94, 98, 103, **103**, 106, 111, **137**
    vases/bottles 106, 108, 111

grooms **3**, 72–5, **72**, **74–5**

hair 50–9, **50**
    adornments 50, 52, **52–3**, 55, 81
    beehives 53, **54**, 56
    styles 53, **53–5**, 55–6, 75
    and veils 49
headdresses *see* veils and headdresses
Hettie Rose Limited 34–5, 36–7
Hope and Harlequin 22–3
hosiery 27, **27**

ice cream tables 128, 131, **131**
inspiration 134–9, **134**, **137**

jackets 74, **74**, 75
jewellery 66–71, **66**, **68–9**
    bouquets made of 108
    bracelets **68**, 70, **70–1**
    brooches 66, 69, 70–1
    earrings 7, **68**, 70, **70**
    necklaces **4**, 18, 41, 68, 70–1
Joanna Millington Photography 115–17

kimonos, vintage 35, 36–7

lavender bags 99
letterpress print 84, **84**, 86
lighting **100**
lingerie 24–9, **24–6**
    basques 26, 29
    corsets 29
    girdles 29
    structured 26
    unstructured 27
locations 88–93, **88**
    country barns/halls 91–2, **91**
    exteriors 96
    finding 90
    and flowers 110
    grand houses 92–3, **92–3**
    homespun 90–1
    retro chic 93, **93**
Love Blooms 108, 110–11
LovebySusie 41, 48–9

macaroons 6
make-up 60–5, **60**, **62–3**
marquees 91
message tables 132, **132**
music 124–7, **124**, **126–7**

photo booths 115
photos 112–17, **112**, **114–15**
picnic-style areas 96, 97
place settings 98–9, 102, **102**
Powderpuff Girls 62, 64–5
proposals 5
pudding tables 130, **130**

seating plans 132, **132**
shirts 72, 74, 75, **75**
shoes **3**, 18, 30–7, **30**, **32–3**, **35**, **138**
    decorations 34–5
    designing your own 35, 36
    dyeing 32–3
    groom's 74, 75
    shoe clips 34
    vintage-inspired 32, 36–7
stationery 82–7, **82**, **84–5**
suits 74, 75, **75**
sweet tables 130, **130**

table touches 6, 7, **94**, 98, **98–9**, 102–3, **102–3**, 106, 111, **137**
ties **3**, 72, 74–5, **74–5**
trousers **3**, 75

veils and headdresses 8, 38–49, **38**, **40–2**, **46–7**
    birdcage veils **38**, 41, **41**, 43
    caps **38**, 48
    dyeing veils 47
    fascinators 44, **44**
    feather headdresses 45, **45**
    flower crowns 40, 44, **44**
    and hairstyles 59
    hats **3**, 41, **41**
    headbands 42, **42**
    reviving veils 45–6
    traditional veils 40–1
    veil styles 43
Vintage Wedding Dress Company, The 12–13

waistcoats **3**, 72, 74, 75
wedding planners 97
What Katie Did 26, 28–9, 79

A DAVID & CHARLES BOOK
© F&W Media International, Ltd 2013

David & Charles is an imprint of F&W Media International, Ltd
Brunel House, Forde Close, Newton Abbot, TQ12 4PU, UK

F&W Media International, Ltd is a subsidiary of F+W Media, Inc.,
10151 Carver Road, Cincinnati OH45242, USA

Text and designs copyright © Lucy Morris 2013
Layout and Photography © F&W Media International, Ltd 2013

First published in the UK and US in 2013

A catalogue record for this book is available from the British Library.

ISBN-13: 978-1-4463-0357-3 Hardback
ISBN-10: 1-4463-0357-8 Hardback

ISBN-13: 978-1-4463-0358-0 Paperback
ISBN-10: 1-4463-0358-6 Paperback

Printed in China by RR Donnelley for:
F&W Media International, Ltd
Brunel House, Forde Close, Newton Abbot, TQ12 4PU, UK

10 9 8 7 6 5 4 3 2 1

Publisher: Alison Myer
Junior Acquisitions Editor: Verity Graves-Morris
Project Editor: Lin Clements
Senior Designer: Victoria Marks
Photographer: Joanna Millington
Production Manager: Bev Richardson

Illustrations by Chrsitina Morris and Lucy Morris

F+W Media publishes high quality books on a wide range of subjects.
For more great book ideas visit: www.rucraft.co.uk